MW00825278

Reading & writing
with English Learners

a framework for K–5

Valentina Gonzalez
& Melinda Miller

Published by Seidlitz Education
P.O. Box 166827
Irving, TX 75016
www.seidlitzeducation.com

Copyright © 2020 Seidlitz Education

No part of this book may be reproduced in any form or by electronic or mechanical means, including photocopy, recording, scanning, or other, without prior permission from the publisher.

To obtain permission to use material from this work, please submit a written request to Seidlitz Education Permissions Department, P.O. Box 166827, Irving, TX 75016

For related titles and support materials visit www.seidlitzeducation.com.

10.20

Contents

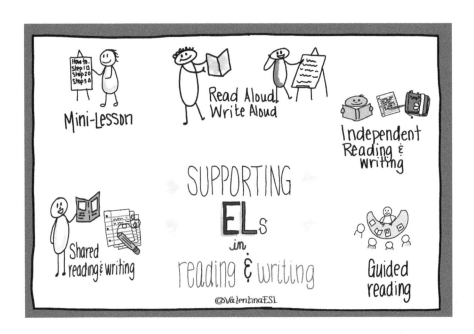

Introduction

Hello from Valentina & Melinda

This book grew out of the love we both have for students, teaching, and literacy. We both recognize the unique needs that students have, and we wish to honor them in the work we do. We also know and value the work teachers do in classrooms, and we want to be a support for educators.

Whether your school and district embraces a workshop approach to reading and writing or you have a program you follow, we believe that the methods shared in this resource will help you as you work with your students. These methods are not meant to replace the literacy base that you currently have but rather to enhance the work you do with students. We hope you will be able to apply what is written here to your current teaching context.

As we wrote this book, we tried to consider a variety of stakeholders, including readers, educators, and students. We take this work very seriously, and even though we know that our views on pedagogy may differ from other perspectives, we know that we all want what's best for students.

The need for a resource such as this one came to our attention through our work with teachers of English learners (ELs). As the number of ELs is increasing, teachers are looking for ways to meet their students' literacy needs. We both advocate a strengths-based perspective that views the assets, background, and literacy of each English learner as a starting point from which educators can build.

We advocate and believe that English learners should receive systematic, explicit English language development instruction from ESL/ESOL-certified teachers in addition to accommodated and scaffolded language arts general education classroom instruction. While we recognize that teaching ESL/ESOL and teaching language arts are not the same, many ideas in this book will help teachers in both settings.

This book aims to support you as a teacher of literacy and language and in increasing student success and progress, regardless of your context. Feel free to use this book any way you wish. Read it cover to cover or just read the chapters you would like to know more about.

We have both seen the methods we describe throughout the book lead to success for so many English learners in our own classrooms and other teachers' classrooms, and we are

excited to share our stories and describe what has worked for our students. We hope you will be able to add some of the ideas in this book to your repertoire of effective techniques.

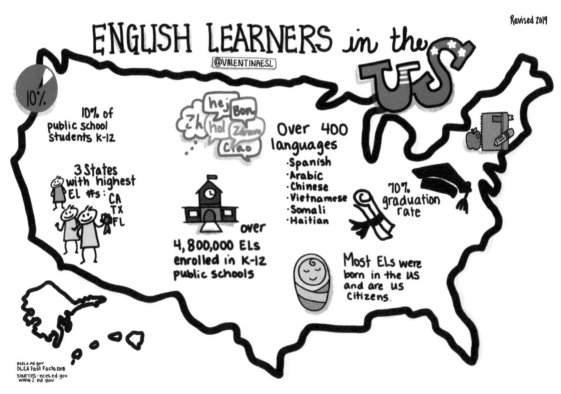

A Note from Valentina

I am filled to the brim with happiness to write a book about two things I love so much: English learners and literacy. English is my second language, and as a young student, I didn't exactly fall in love with reading and writing. In elementary school, I couldn't connect with books like I later taught my own students to do.

When I became an English teacher and then an ESL teacher, it became my passion and challenge to make reading and writing a priority for the students I served. Engaging students, instilling a joy and love of reading and writing, and helping them find their passions became my mission.

Over the years, I taught with scripted programs using basal readers, and later I implemented a workshop model in my classroom. As I experienced teaching with a variety of structures, I increasingly noticed that my English learners had unique and specific needs. Learning to accommodate my instruction to maximize their language and literacy development was key to helping them achieve success.

One thing I noticed throughout the years as a teacher of both general education and ESL was that so much professional learning happens in silos. When I was a main-stream teacher, rarely did I receive professional development about teaching English learners. The professional development I was asked to attend was centered around the curriculum of reading and writing. We learned about the programs that were available to us, the resources we could use, and how to teach the subjects of reading and writing in general. But my training seemed to lack guidance on how to accommodate and differentiate for the needs of diverse learners. Although my ESL students spent more time with me than with a specialized ESL teacher, I wasn't sure how to provide them with the necessary scaffolds they needed to make progress. And that scared me.

Then, when I became an ESL teacher, I noticed that I was not getting much training anymore in content areas such as reading and writing. This concerned me because I was still serving the same students and supporting their academic growth along with their linguistic growth.

Looking back from the outside, what I see is a disconnect. When I began working in professional development, my focus became creating connections for general education and ESL teachers. I wanted to empower all teachers who work with English learners by giving them the tools they need to better serve students.

So if you are a mainstream teacher, you are welcome here. This is a book that will support you as you work with all students but specifically with students who are learning English as a second or other language. And if you are an ESL teacher, this book is for you, too! This book will help you as you think about your ESL students through a literacy lens.

A Note from Melinda

I have always been a writer. I wrote my first book when I was in first grade, and I called it "A Book of My Cats." Little did I realize that my second grade sister and I participated in the writing process every day after school. We went home and excitedly ran to our shared room, chattering about what we wanted to write about that day. We told each other stories and talked about what we were going to write—that was our prewriting. We wrote our cat stories in composition books for our drafting step. We added things to make our stories more exciting or different from each other's stories, and that was our revising. Then we asked our mom and dad to help us spell things we didn't yet know how to spell, and we fixed them. That was editing. We illustrated our stories and copied them into our final drafts—publishing.

We read them to each other, we took them to school for show-and-tell, and we read them to our parents. When our grandparents came to visit, we ran to greet them, books in hand, ready to read to them before they even set their suitcases down. We were excited to write, and we had our own little community of writers. Unfortunately, that only happened at home. In school, we had to write two-line stories, and they had to be written in our best handwriting and spelled correctly from the get-go. If something needed to be fixed, we erased, made holes in our papers, and got in trouble. I found no joy in writing time at school. I always felt like whatever I did wasn't good enough. I just couldn't wait to get home again and write with my sister.

When I became a teacher, I wanted my students to find joy in reading and writing. I wanted them to have experiences like I had writing at home—not the ones I had at school. During my second year of teaching, I learned about the writing process and Writing Workshop and began to implement both in my classroom. I soon discovered that I had learned to write

through the writing process at home. I wanted my students to experience the joy I'd experienced as I began to see myself as a writer through my at-home writing experiences. I did not want them to experience the frustration of having to produce perfect writing that lacked meaning. I'd always been excited to write about my cats because they were a big part of my life at home, and I knew it was important for students, especially English learners, to write about what they know and what they love. Writing Workshop was the answer! In implementing this strategy, I found that all my students, including English learners, happily planned and wrote their stories then excitedly made them into books!

> Writing Workshop is the perfect environment for students to learn at their own rate.

Throughout my years of teaching first and second grade, I saw many students blossom as young writers in my classroom through Writing Workshop and the writing process. Writing Workshop is the perfect environment for students to learn at their own rate. Students needed different amounts of scaffolding from me. For example, some English learners I taught needed modeling and support from pictures as they learned what it was like to participate in the writing process. One boy in particular, Lionel, needed me to take dictation from him as he wrote his first couple of pieces. Later, he was able to create stories on his own. I found that every student could be successful in the Writing Workshop with the right amount of support. Some students could write three-page stories, books about dinosaurs, or poetry. Others were learning to think about sounds and represent those sounds with letters, and they used mostly drawings to convey meaning in their stories. All of these students found a home in our community of writers, and they supported each other as they all became authors.

In addition to Writing Workshop, I also implemented the other components of a balanced literacy approach in my classroom. I found that English learners thrived in our language-rich classroom. In shared reading, for example, English learners were able to listen to students around them and participate in the reading at their own level in a safe environment while they were learning English.

Write-Aloud and shared writing were also very helpful for English learners in my classroom. As I modeled the writing for them, they were able to see the writing process and talk to their peers and ask questions of me. Then they were able to participate in shared writing at their own levels to contribute to the class story. When it was time for independent writing, they wrote at their own paces and their own levels, frequently drawing pictures to go with their stories. Through implementing a balanced approach to literacy in my classroom, I watched many English learners thrive as I was able to cater to their needs and scaffold their learning.

I, too, am filled with joy as Valentina and I write this book. Throughout the pages, we provide our ideas for helping children become proficient readers and writers. We include what has worked for us with all students, especially English learners. What we discuss in the following pages is what we consider to be the best plan for teaching literacy to all students. While you don't have to do things exactly the way we recommend in this book, we hope you will find something you can use to help your students become the best they can be.

We hope your students will find joy as they become readers and writers!

Our Core Beliefs About Teaching Reading & Writing to English Learners

English learners benefit from multiple opportunities to read, write, listen, and speak with their peers throughout the day.

Literacy in any language holds value and can be leveraged to support learning English.

The use of a student's primary language is valuable in the classroom.

All children should see themselves in the literature and on the walls of the classroom.

Student choice in reading and writing is essential.

Students need plenty of time for reading and writing practice.

The use of culturally inclusive texts is necessary to create a welcoming classroom environment.*

*For a list of books to get you started, see page 128.

Chapter 1

Implementing a Balanced Approach to Literacy

"People are always looking for the single *magic bullet* that will totally change everything. There is no single magic bullet."

— Temple Grandin

The sense of urgency when teaching English learners (ELs) is significant. ELs are learning to read and write in English while learning the academic language of the content at the same time. The goal of this book is to share research-based instructional methods that increase English learners' academic success. The book will outline a balanced approach to literacy, integrating reading and writing components that are linguistically accommodated. This book is designed to help you as you support English learners' language development, literacy skills, and academic growth.

But before we tell you how, we need to tell you why. The following pages will provide a brief but thorough overview of the research that lays the groundwork for implementing a balanced approach to literacy.

To begin, it should come as no surprise that there are varying perspectives on teaching reading and writing. The controversy surrounding the whole language versus phonics approach to reading is nothing new. While some believe that teaching word parts explicitly is fundamental, others believe that readers should simply be immersed in literature. In addition, some argue that reading is the act of decoding while others believe that reading is making meaning of text. Ever since the National Reading Panel (2000) found that a combination of both of these approaches seems to benefit readers, educators have been seeking the right balance. In fact, knowing the right balance is essential.

THE ROOTS OF BALANCED LITERACY: A BRIEF HISTORY

A traditional classroom in the 1960s and 1970s could be described as a skills-based or phonics-based classroom. Depending upon your age, many of you may remember reading instruction in the form of reading groups using basal readers. Typically, a basal reader is leveled and comes with a teacher's guide with scripted or suggested lessons. Readers within the group take turns reading, round-robin style. Phonics skills instruction comes in the form of workbooks designed to go with the basal reader and worksheets provided by the teacher. You may also remember a classroom where there was a focus on handwriting and spelling, or you might remember writing a two- or three-line story on lined paper and drawing a picture to go with it in a large, blank section at the top of the page.

During the 1970s and 1980s, many researchers began to look at learning to read, write, listen, and speak as "literacy learning," rather than as isolated events (Clay, 1979, 1982, 1985, 1991; Teale & Sulzby, 1986; Cooper, 2000). The writings of Vygotsky (1978) described how children learn socially while being supported by an adult or by peers. In addition, Halliday (1975) introduced the notion that children learn holistically and not piece by piece. Whole language came into being as a result of these ideas (Cooper, 2000). Students in a whole language classroom learn to read and write by actually reading and writing. The teacher provides skill and strategy instruction through mini-lessons.

Delpit (1986, 1995) suggested that teachers of whole language and phonics/skills-based instruction have something to say to each other. She explained that when she began teaching with a whole language approach in Philadelphia, her white, middle-class students succeeded, but her minority students lagged behind. She realized her minority students needed more direct teaching of phonics, reading strategies, and writing techniques, as well as time to practice the orchestration of their new learning through authentic reading and writing. Delpit stressed the need for a combination of whole language and skills-based instruction.

Wright (2015) describes a balanced approach to literacy as one that "recognizes the need for some direct instruction in reading skills but emphasizes the importance of providing such instruction in meaningful contexts to ensure that students are able to comprehend and use what they read for authentic purposes" (p. 183).

In the 1990s, researchers began to emphasize that there was not just one right way to teach literacy (Cooper, 2000), and that a balanced approach was essential in order to ensure all students receive the instruction they needed. The balanced literacy approach, according to Snow, Burns, and Griffin (1998), combines explicit strategy and skill instruction with meaningful daily reading and writing experiences in order to allow students time to practice orchestrating reading and writing skills. Balanced literacy instruction combines the whole language and skills-based approaches to ensure all students experience the literacy instruction they need to succeed.

Wright (2015) describes a balanced approach to literacy as one that "recognizes the need for some direct instruction in reading skills but emphasizes the importance of providing such instruction in meaningful contexts to ensure that students are able to comprehend and use what they read for authentic purposes" (p. 183). "Direct instruction" in this case does not mean drill and kill, worksheets, or memorization of information. Instead, teachers scaffold students' understanding through modeling, mini-lessons, role-play, conferences, strategy instruction, and word work while ensuring that students have many meaningful experiences with authentic text. In a balanced approach to literacy, the focus is on making meaning and on comprehending.

A balanced approach to literacy offers a comprehensive language and literacy framework in which the teacher uses a variety of approaches that meet students' learning needs. This can be highly effective for English learners since they are learning language while also learning content. Teachers in a balanced literacy classroom provide comprehensible input for English learners (Krashen, 1981). Comprehensible input is "any written or spoken message that is understandable to a language learner because of the context" (Salva & Matis, 2017, p. 45). In Krashen's theory of second language acquisition, the focus is on providing input that is comprehensible but slightly challenging for the student. If a language learner receives no challenge at all, it is difficult to grow in language development. On the other hand, if the input is too challenging, the learner would not be able to understand.

Aural comprehensible input can be provided by the teacher, a native language peer, or media. Teachers use clear, simplified speech that matches the students' proficiency levels and avoid idioms or colloquialisms when delivering comprehensible input. When using media for comprehensible input, teachers find sources of media that are exciting and match the students' interests. For written comprehensible input, teachers provide high-interest text from which students can choose and ensure students receive appropriate context and native language support (Seidlitz, 2019).

The teacher can adjust instruction to meet individual students where they are. Students who are acquiring the English language will need scaffolds and accommodations to support comprehension and advance literacy.

A balanced literacy approach also provides many opportunities for comprehensible output through conversation, writing, reading, drama, presentations, and endless other experiences (Swain, 1985, 1995). Salva and Matis (2017) create opportunities for students to participate in output that "honor(s) their intelligence and their unique perspectives" (p. 52). The beauty of the balanced approach to literacy is that students respond to instruction in ways that are meaningful and motivating to them.

According to Herrera and Murry (2011), English learners should have many opportunities for authentic and rich literacy experiences throughout their language development. In addition, the authors emphasize that English learners should be able to "maximize their own prior experiences, culture, background knowledge, and reasoning" within the literacy classroom (p.72). The balanced literacy approach provides authentic reading and writing experiences that allow English learners to build on their background knowledge and read and write about topics that interest them and topics they know about.

Cooper and Kiger (2003) describe a balanced literacy classroom as incorporating reading and writing instruction with reading and writing practice. *Students must have a sustained time every day to practice their reading and writing and apply the skills and strategies they are learning.* In addition, the authors stress the importance of including gradual release of responsibility through read-aloud, shared reading, guided reading, and independent reading, as well as write-aloud, shared writing, and independent writing.

MISCONCEPTIONS ABOUT BALANCED LITERACY

As we stated before, there are many different ideas when it comes to reading and writing instruction. There are some that perceive balanced literacy to mean a "little bit of this and a little bit of that" but not enough of anything. Others claim that the term "balanced literacy" is used loosely to define instruction that puts everything in all at once. There are misconceptions that balanced literacy is an independent free-for-all where students read and write freely with little direct or explicit instruction. However, in a balanced approach to literacy, teachers serve students with a "well-rounded, balanced diet of literacy" (Calkins, 2015, p. 27). Cunningham and Allington (2011) even compare balanced literacy to a multivitamin. Teachers combine explicit instruction, guided practice, and daily time for independent reading and writing to cater to the needs of each learner (Tompkins, 2015). Rather than "a little bit of this and a little bit of that," teachers try various methods in order to find the specific method that works for each individual student.

The International Literacy Association (ILA) defines balanced literacy this way:

A balanced literacy program includes both foundational and language comprehension instructional features, such as phonemic awareness and phonics (understanding the relationships between sounds and their written representations), fluency, guided oral reading, vocabulary development, and comprehension. An alternative interpretation of balanced literacy is that it mixes features of whole language and basic skills instruction. (ILA, n.d.)

Many educators feel that the combination of decoding and making meaning is necessary

for literacy. Knowing the research about what works for students, educators can use a balanced approach to literacy to pull from the "strongest elements of whole language and phonics instruction" (Salva & Matis, 2017, p. 74).

In a July 2019 blog post, Sawchuk discusses a recent brief put out by ILA, endorsing the teaching of systematic and explicit phonics in early grades. They state, "systematic phonics means that students are exposed to each sound-letter pattern in the English language in turn. Explicit means that those patterns are directly taught by teachers, not 'discovered' via indirect prompting or inquiry activities." Sawchuk and Schwartz go on to quote Marcie Post, ILA's executive director, as saying, "We're talking about an integrated approach between the teaching of phonics and literature. There is a need for explicit instruction, but you can't teach meaning-making on a phonics curriculum alone." These statements from the blog post strengthen the notion that a balanced approach to literacy should include both direct teaching of skills

such as phonics and time for students to practice the use of these strategies and skills through the reading of authentic literature.

Cooper and Kiger (2003) describe a balanced literacy classroom as incorporating reading and writing instruction with reading and writing practice. Students must have a sustained time every day to practice their reading and writing and apply the skills and strategies they are learning. In addition, the authors stress the importance of including gradual release of responsibility through read-aloud, shared reading, guided reading, and independent reading, as well as write-aloud, shared writing, and independent writing. A popular way of meeting the goals of a balanced literacy classroom has been the workshop model, originally attributed to Donald Graves (1983) and further developed by Lucy Calkins (1986). This book will focus on how to help ELs be successful through this approach.

Workshop teaching is a structure. It is not a program or script.

A WORKSHOP MODEL

When thinking about what's important in a literacy- and language-rich environment that promotes both academic and linguistic progress, ask yourself these questions:

• Is a gradual release of responsibility important? For example, do you believe in reading and writing to, with, and by English learners?

• To what degree do you consider whole group instruction, small group instruction, and individual application important?

• What is the role of reading aloud to students?

• Where does modeling of writing and shared writing fit into your work with students?

• How do we meet students where they are instructionally and help them grow from there?

A workshop approach to reading and writing can help us answer these questions in a way that authentically meets the needs of our English learners. Many literacy teachers implement a workshop structure for reading and writing as part of their balanced approach to literacy.

Typically, reading workshop includes mini-lessons, teacher read-aloud, shared reading, guided reading, and independent reading, though all components are not necessarily used in one day. According to Tompkins (2015), reading workshop "fosters real reading of self-selected books..." (p. 305).

Students read authentic texts, and they receive support and guidance from the teacher. Cooper (2000) states that reading workshop is an effective method for reading instruction in the balanced literacy classroom. Within the reading workshop, English learners are supported and nurtured as they learn to read, talk about text with their peers, and participate in guided, shared, and independent reading.

Writing Workshop is based upon the writing process, which includes planning, drafting, editing, revising, and publishing a final product with guidance and instruction from the teacher. According to Echevarria and Graves (2003), writers workshop has been helpful for many students, including those who have had difficulty with writing.

The workshop structure is particularly beneficial to English learners because it meets the following criteria:
Follows a routine
Uses familiar language
Offers choice in reading and writing
Provides small group and individual instruction
Builds on students' assets and prior knowledge

Workshop Structure

Workshop teaching is a structure. It is not a program or script. Workshops typically include the following elements:

Mini Lesson
5-10 min of whole group, explicit instruction.

Independent Time
20-45 min of choice reading/writing. Sometimes with a partner. This is also when the teacher gathers small groups or confers with students.

Share Time
Final 5-10 min. Students share what they've learned with a partner or whole group.

How does the approach look different in grades K through 2 versus grades 3 through 5?

All primary and elementary students need a sustained time every day to read and write in authentic ways while learning skills and strategies to help them read and write. In the primary years of school, kindergarten through second grade, as students work diligently on learning to read and breaking the code, we establish the foundations of literacy. In these early years, it is important to give students many literacy experiences and surround them with print. The focus may be on phonemic awareness, alphabetic principle, alphabetic code, and the written code. Students at this age are learning reading and writing strategies, learning to decode text in order to read, and learning to create text through writing. As they begin to read and write, students learn to use cueing systems (semantic, structural, and graphophonic cues) to make sense of the text as well as to create text. Some students, including many English learners, need strategy instruction to help them learn to use the cueing systems (Clay, 1993). This is important work that takes time and should not be rushed, because students'

future literacy achievement depends on it. The workshop format is excellent for the typical primary classroom that has English learners as well as native English speakers at many different levels. Teachers can focus on strategy instruction during mini-lessons, small group instruction time, or conferences with individuals.

As students move into the intermediate grades, third through fifth, they face increasingly challenging "cognitive and linguistic demands" in reading and should address "decoding skills, language development and competence, concept and context building, and critical thinking skills and strategies" (Sutton, 1989, p. 684, 685) within the context of language and literature. Students begin to apply and transfer the literacy and language skills they've acquired in their own personal reading and writing lives. Some students at this level, particularly English learners, may be emergent readers and writers. Students who have not mastered phonemic awareness, phonics, and reading and writing strategies in intermediate grades can be provided the instruction they need through small groups, individual conferencing, and independent reading or writing time.

Teachers can create a literacy-rich classroom, provide many authentic reading and writing experiences for students, and support and encourage them as they become readers and writers. The beauty of Reading & Writing Workshop is that students are able to work at their own pace and at their own level. While some students work independently, others can work one-on-one with the teacher or in small groups to receive targeted instruction that meets their personalized needs. During independent reading and writing time, some teachers choose to provide stations or centers for students to rotate through while they meet with small groups or confer with individual students. This is especially common as students build stamina in reading and writing independently.

How Do I Get Started? When I first began teaching, I was handed a large white binder. I was told it held all of the reading and writing curriculum I needed to teach for the year. It was the biggest, most overwhelming binder I had ever laid eyes on. Obviously, this dates me. Along with my curriculum binder was a set of spiral-bound basal texts. Each week, I met with my grade-level language arts partners to plan. We flipped through the pages of the large teacher's editions, and we planned out our whole group lessons. We read class novels, and everyone did the same thing. One size had to fit all.

Fast forward a few years: I began hearing about balanced literacy at professional development trainings, and I started to wonder if what I was doing was effective for all of my students. But I was scared. How could I change what I was doing? What if it didn't work? What if I did it wrong? Change sounded difficult.

As I learned more about the components of balanced literacy, I realized why it was better for my students. I found that I already had some of the components in my instruction. And most importantly, I realized that I needed to meet my students where they were, not serve them from a random place in the curriculum. I had always believed that students came first. Balanced literacy fit right in.

— *Valentina*

My story is quite similar to Valentina's. My first two years of teaching, I used the lessons provided in the basal reader's teacher's edition. The students read the same things and worked on the same workbook pages and worksheets. Again, it was definitely a one-size-fits-all situation.

My third year of teaching, our district hired a new assistant superintendent who mixed things up by introducing the balanced literacy approach to our district. Gone were the basals, worksheets, and workbooks. He introduced Reading & Writing Workshop to us and provided books and writing supplies for all of our students. He also emphasized that students must learn skills through mini-lessons, small group instruction, and conferences, and that those skills must be taught through the context of reading and writing and come from authentic need that is based upon the students' work.

The assistant superintendent also encouraged read-aloud and "Drop Everything and Read." He taught us about write-aloud and shared reading and writing, as well as guided reading. He frequently provided us with professional development and sent expert teachers to our classrooms to demonstrate how to do Writing Workshop and guided reading.

I was teaching second grade at the time, and the kids in my class that year would graduate high school in the year 2000. Because of the special year they would graduate, the assistant superintendent came and read to all second grade classes that year about once a month. My students and I were introduced to some of the best picture books ever written, and we were always excited to hear the talent and enthusiasm with which he read.

Though many teachers at my district were dragged into balanced literacy kicking and screaming, being a fairly new teacher, I bought into it right away. My students were excited and loved the freedom to choose what they read and what they wrote about. Literacy started to make sense to them. Students were able to work at their own level and pace, and I was able to work one-on-one with many students, including English learners, to provide the support they needed. We all found joy in literacy that year, and I felt like I had been born again as a teacher!

— Melinda

Here are the steps to implementing your own balanced literacy approach

1. Understand the components.
Understanding the balanced literacy approach and why it is beneficial for students is critical. The more you know about each piece of the puzzle, the stronger your implementation will be. One thing we have found over the years is that having common vocabulary and definitions among teammates, campus and/or district wide, makes a difference. For example, the more we can be on the same page about what shared reading is and is not, the better we can administer it effectively throughout.

2. Look at what you already have in place.
If you are new to balanced literacy, once you understand what the components are, you will realize that you may have already implemented many of them. You may already be reading aloud to your class and providing independent reading. Furthermore, you may also be supporting students through small-group instruction or delivering whole-group instruction through mini-lessons.

3. Identify what's missing.
While you may already be implementing lots of strategies, when you reflect on your experiences in the classroom, you may notice that something particular is missing. For example, if your typical lesson includes you delivering instruction and students completing a worksheet, reading a text, or writing in their journals, your weak area may be modeling how to read and write through shared experiences. With a little additional structure and reflection, you'll be ensuring that you provide shared opportunities for your students. An effective way to start this type of reflection is to ask yourself this basic question:
What components of balanced literacy am I missing?

4. Learn more.
After recognizing the power of a balanced approach to literacy and how we could differentiate instruction for all of our students, we both craved more information. We wanted to refine this craft. Both of us sought out district-provided professional development, read books on the topic, and learned from colleagues. In fact, one of the most powerful (and readily available) training opportunities is to learn from an ESL co-teacher. Inviting a co-teacher into your room can open up many learning opportunities for both of you. You can even tag-team or double up on providing balanced literacy, with one of you pulling guided reading groups and the other conferring with independent readers. We believe wholeheartedly that learning never ends and that we can always grow.

INSIDE THIS BOOK

In an effort to give you a glimpse of how to support English learners within language arts lessons, throughout the book we will reference three general education classrooms in a suburban school.

Grade Level	Teacher	Number of Students	Demographics
1st	Ms. Montrose	22 kids	6 ELs: 2 Beginning, 3 Intermediate, 1 Advanced
3rd	Mr. Menil	22 kids	3 ELs: 1 Beginning, 2 Advanced
5th	Ms. Dunlavy	26 kids	4 ELs: 1 Beginning, 1 Intermediate, 1 Advanced, 1 Nearly Fluent

Much like instruction in classrooms with students, we organized this book into sections based on specific reading and writing activities with a Gradual Release of Responsibility in mind (see p. 23). We move from having the teacher do the bulk of the work in the Mini-Lesson and Read-Aloud to working together in Shared Reading and Guided Reading and finally to having students work independently with Independent Reading. Next, we move into Writing and follow a similar Gradual Release structure with Write-Aloud, Shared Writing, and Independent Writing.

In each chapter we take a literacy component and break it down in the following way:

What It Is
This section will provide an overview that will define the component and give a brief description.

What It's Not
This section will aim to clear up any misconceptions about what the component might look like and sound like.

The Benefits for English Learners
Here we will outline what English learners specifically gain from the implementation of the component and why it is valuable.

Accommodating for English Learners
This section will give powerful ways to support English learners and maximize instruction.

Classroom Scenario

The classroom scenarios will give you a peek inside a classroom that serves English learners through a balanced approach to literacy.

What the Experts Say

Here we will offer relevant and recent research from respected authorities in the field.

Frequently Asked Questions

In this section we will discuss common questions from the field with practical answers that will support you as you serve English learners in a workshop setting.

A Lesson Map

Here we will outline the essential steps to implement the component into your work with students. Each lesson map includes icons that indicate when students are listening, speaking, reading, and writing.

 Listening

 Speaking

 Reading

 Writing

It is our hope that, as you read, you feel validated in the powerful work you are doing with English learners and also that you find new ways to grow and develop your instruction as a model of language and literacy for English learners.

Take a moment to reflect on the Temple Grandin quote at the beginning of this chapter. She said there is no single magic bullet. That is why we must try many things until we find out what works for each individual learner. You might not consider yourself a reading/Writing Workshop teacher, yet we invite you to use the techniques within the pages of this book. The balanced approach to literacy provides a context in which teachers are able to implement a variety of strategies with individual students or small groups while other students work independently. This is the perfect environment for meeting English learners where they are, finding out what they need, and adapting instruction to meet those needs. We hope you will find something in this book that will help each and every one of your students become successful readers, writers, listeners, and speakers.

Chapter 2

Mini-Lesson

> "Reading and writing *float* on a sea of talk"
> — James Britton

WHAT IS A MINI-LESSON?

The mini-lesson is a critical component of a language-rich classroom. It sets students off on the right path for the rest of the class period. This is a laser-focused 10 to 15 minutes of targeted, explicit instruction with the whole group. The teacher gathers students in front of the board or presentation area and introduces one specific skill, concept, or strategy. Students learn in a safe, guided setting while the teacher monitors for understanding.

According to Fountas and Pinnell (2001), there are three categories of mini-lessons:
• Lessons on management
• Lessons on strategies and skills
• Lessons on literary analysis

The main purpose of the mini-lesson is to deliver a skill, concept, or strategy to the whole group in one short, focused time frame. In this way, all students hear and experience the same message. In the Gradual Release of Responsibility model, instruction can be divided into three phases: I DO, WE DO, and YOU DO (Pearson & Gallagher, 1983). The mini-lesson is a component of I DO because this is where explicit modeling of instruction takes place. Following the mini-lesson, students move to reading or writing independently as the teacher pulls and confers with small groups. Students are reminded to apply the new concept to their reading and/or writing.

There are many structures for a mini-lesson. One that works well for English learners was created by Lucy Calkins (2000) from the Teachers College Reading and Writing Project. As you can see below, this mini-lesson follows a specific structure that ensures that the lesson is kept clear and concise. It also allows for a nice routine that students are able to rely on as they move through the language arts block regardless of whether or not the classroom holds a workshop structure.

A typical mini-lesson might follow this format:

Connection: Bridging the new learning to something students have already learned

Teaching: Stating the new learning

Active Engagement: Providing students with time to practice

Link: Reminding students when and how this will be useful in everyday life

The mini Lesson
@ValentineESL

connection

teaching

active engagement

link

WHAT A MINI-LESSON IS NOT

Mini-lessons are not lengthy lectures with little to no student interaction. They are not a time for PowerPoint presentations. It may seem tempting to use a PowerPoint to guide a mini-lesson; however, it is not recommended. Instead, this short lesson is more effective when the teacher models the new strategy on the spot and creates an anchor chart in front of the class. Rather than having specific time for questions and answers, teachers are encouraged to include or plan specific structures that will enable the students to have their questions answered and be actively engaged. The teacher is not the only one doing the talking. For example, students could engage by turning to discuss with a partner, acting out a scene, or trying out the strategy that the teacher demonstrated.

Gradual Release of Responsibility & Components of Literacy

I do	We do	You do
★ Mini-Lesson	• Shared Reading	• Independent Reading
• Read-Aloud	• Guided Reading	• Independent Writing
• Write-Aloud	• Shared Writing	
explicit & modeled	structured & supported	automatic & natural

Component of the Mini-Lesson	Benefit for English Learners
Connection	• Activates prior knowledge • Builds background
Teaching	• Offers explicit, concise instruction • Models effective skills or strategies • Includes clear demonstration
Active Engagement	• Offers practice of reading, writing, or speaking • Allows peer-to-peer interaction
Link	• Provides real-world application and transfer of knowledge

THE BENEFITS OF MINI-LESSONS FOR ENGLISH LEARNERS

The mini-lesson is short in nature, focusing less on teacher talk and more on student interaction or practice. The longer the whole-group instruction is, the less time students have to practice reading, writing, and speaking (Bigelman & Peterson, 2016). Let's examine each piece of the mini-lesson for its specific benefits for ELs.

English learners at earlier levels of proficiency in English particularly benefit from the explicit instruction of the mini-lesson. In addition, gathering the class in one group fosters a sense of community and is an excellent opportunity to weave in culturally responsive components. By coupling the mini-lesson with text that is inclusive and represents the students you teach, you can build empathy and compassion in your classroom community. Mini-lessons provide an opportunity for us to model reading and writing skills, concepts, and strategies. Modeling for students is an effective way to show them how proficient readers and writers navigate print.

ACCOMMODATING THE MINI-LESSON FOR ENGLISH LEARNERS

Mini-lessons may not be easily accessible to all students, including English learners. However, we can accommodate our mini-lessons in a few subtle ways to ensure that they meet the needs of all students and don't become "wastes of time" for some.

Here are some suggestions for accommodating the mini-lesson:

- Create anchor charts with the class
- Use gestures
- Speak clearly and at a natural rate
- Add visuals
- Embed opportunities for peer interaction
- Offer sentence stems
- Check for understanding
- Tap into the assets and culture of the students you serve
- Use structured conversation moves during the active engagement

Mini-lessons are pathways to successful independent reading and writing for students. The mini-lesson allows teachers time to share, model, and "think aloud" about the most important skills, strategies, and concepts that benefit all readers and writers. Let's take a look at this classroom scenario.

Mr. Menil has gathered his third grade class together in the common area. He asked each of them to bring a fiction book they recently finished reading on their own. Out of his 22 students, he has three English learners. One is a new immigrant from Guatemala who arrived only a few weeks ago and is at the earliest stages of acquiring English. Two of his English learners are at Advanced levels of English proficiency. Their primary languages are Spanish and Urdu.

Prior to this mini-lesson, Mr. Menil had been conferring with students one-on-one during their independent reading time and also gathering small groups of students to work on guided reading. He took copious notes, and while analyzing those notes, he noticed that a large group of students struggled with finding the theme and lesson. This was a state standard, and Mr. Menil felt his class would benefit from explicit instruction. He decided to plan a mini-lesson that would support students in understanding these concepts, using the story, *Enemy Pie*, by Derek Munson (2000).

Connection

Mr. Menil: *Readers, yesterday I read the story Enemy Pie to you during our read-aloud time. We all enjoyed that story, and we made many connections to our own lives. But then I went home, and I started thinking about the main character and the changes he went through throughout the book. I started to really wonder about what caused those changes, and then that made me wonder about this big question: What did I learn based on those changes? What was the author trying to teach me? When characters change, that's often a sign that there's something new we can learn about them. We have to look closely at what characters say, think, or do.*

Mr. Menil uses gestures for "look," "say," "think," and "do." He writes the sentence for students to see. They read it together and use the gestures with Mr. Menil.

Teaching Point

Mr. Menil: *When we read, we can think about characters and how they change to help us understand the lessons authors want us to learn. Let me teach you.*

Teaching

He places the book *Enemy Pie* under the document camera and turns to a show a few pages to the students. As he tracks the text, he demonstrates how the character behaves in the beginning of the book.

Mr. Menil: *Take a look here at the beginning of the book. The main character states clearly that he does not like the new kid in town, Jeremy Ross. He even says that he's created an Enemy List and added Jeremy Ross to it. I can tell by these actions that they are not friends.*

As he talks and refers to the book, Mr. Menil creates an anchor chart in front of the students. Then he turns to a page closer to the end.

Mr. Menil: *But later, they begin to play together. And look here.*

He points to the boys laughing.

Mr. Menil: *They are having a good time. The boys have become friends. So, I think the author is trying to teach us that building relationships can help us make friends.*

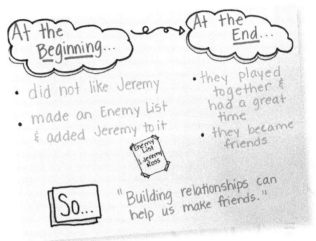

Mr. Menil ends the teaching by reiterating the teaching point using gestures once again.

Mr. Menil: *When we read, we can think about characters and how they change to help us understand the lessons authors want us to learn.*

Active Engagement

Mr. Menil invites students to try finding the themes in their own self-selected fiction books.

Mr. Menil: *You look ready to try this out yourselves! I want you to think about this question.*

Mr. Menil writes the question clearly under the document camera.

Mr. Menil: *'What lesson is the author trying to teach in the book you are reading, and what character changes help you notice this lesson?' When you can answer the question, give me a thumbs up.*

Mr. Menil waits for all thumbs.

Mr. Menil: *Here's how you can respond: "In the book I read called _____, one lesson I noticed was... In the beginning..., but in the end..., so...." Now let's say it all together.*

Mr. Menil and class: *"In the book I read called _____, one lesson I noticed was... In the beginning..., but in the end..., so...."*

Mr. Menil: *Now turn to your partner and share. This time partners with shorter hair can go first. Remember, if you are a listener, your job is important, too. Listen carefully, and ask a question or paraphrase before you share your response.*

Mr. Menil intentionally paired students with partners prior to the mini-lesson. His new student from Guatemala, Josie, is in a triad with a same-language-speaking peer, Manuel, and a native English speaker, Jennifer. This accommodation allows the new student to have linguistic support in her primary language and hear models of English-speaking peers while being included in academic instruction. Let's take a look at what they say to one another.

Jennifer: *"In the book I read called,* Ramona the Pest, *one lesson I noticed was Ramona learned she needed to be good. In the beginning she pulled Susan's hair and got sent home, but in the end she decided she would be good, so she went back to school."*

Manuel: *Oh, my book was the same. In the book I read called,* Click, Clack, Moo Cows that Type, *one lesson I noticed was you have to be nice. In the beginning the farmer wouldn't give the cows any blankets, but in the end they didn't let him have any milk, so he gave them blankets.*

Josie: *In the book I read called* No, David, *one lesson I noticed was you mind Mommy. In the beginning he not mind Mommy, but in the end Mommy give him hug, so he mind Mommy.*

Mr. Menil's Advanced English learners are participating alongside native English-speaking peers with little linguistic support during the mini-lesson. The brevity of the mini-lesson and the opportunity to verbalize with a peer provides these English learners with scaffolds that help them participate. Mr. Menil waits about three minutes until all students have had time to share. During this time, he listens in on students' conversations in an effort to ensure that misconceptions can be cleared up. He gives feedback as needed to groups.

Mr. Menil: *Readers, thank your partners.*

Mr. Menil randomly calls on two or three students and asks them to share either what they said or what their partner said during the peer-to-peer structured conversations.

Link

Mr. Menil: *Readers, there are lessons to be learned in everyday life and in stories that we read. We have to look closely at what characters say, think, and do.*

Mr. Menil points to the sentence, and they read it together, using the gestures with Mr. Menil.

Mr. Menil: *Remember to do this each time you read a story.*

Serravallo (2018) states that "the goal of each mini-lesson is not to give an assignment for the day but rather to offer students a strategy that will become a part of their ongoing reading repertoire" (p. 239).

Intentionally planning a mini-lesson that is clear and concise is vital to the instruction of English learners. "Because English learners lack proficiency and fluency in English, instruction that is not sufficiently explicit, that is vague or indirect, is likely to be confusing or at best not very productive" (Goldenberg & Coleman, 2010, p. 43).

Fountas and Pinnell (2001) remind us that state standards and curriculum guides are references we can lean on for guidance when planning mini-lessons. However, "the real curriculum depends on the particular students you teach. Think about what they already know and use that as your basis for showing them what they need to know next" (p.138). Similarly, Routman (2005) points out that we can "teach into our students' intentions," teaching new concepts our students need when they are ready to use them in their reading or writing (p. 154).

Mini-Lesson Lesson Map

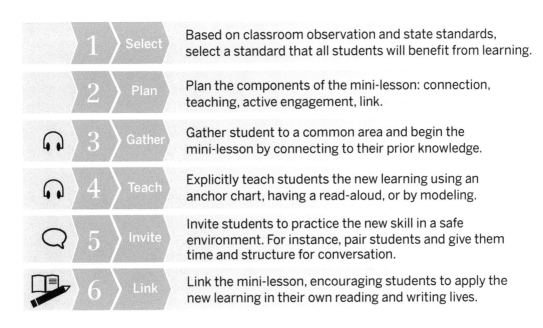

1	Select	Based on classroom observation and state standards, select a standard that all students will benefit from learning.
2	Plan	Plan the components of the mini-lesson: connection, teaching, active engagement, link.
3	Gather	Gather student to a common area and begin the mini-lesson by connecting to their prior knowledge.
4	Teach	Explicitly teach students the new learning using an anchor chart, having a read-aloud, or by modeling.
5	Invite	Invite students to practice the new skill in a safe environment. For instance, pair students and give them time and structure for conversation.
6	Link	Link the mini-lesson, encouraging students to apply the new learning in their own reading and writing lives.

FAQ

How do I determine what to teach during my mini-lesson?

Closely observing your students during independent reading and writing and during small-group instruction will help you to determine the needs of your class. As you work with students, watch closely as they interact with print. As students read, listen in and watch for any commonly missing overarching skills that could benefit the class. Take anecdotal notes during writing conferences, and analyze them later to look for trends. Perhaps the majority of your class has good structure in their writing but lacks the use of transition words. Couple these observations with state standards.

How do I keep my mini-lesson short?

This is important and also difficult for many of us. If you are used to lecturing or teaching for longer periods of time, keeping the mini-lesson short might take time. We have had luck with two strategies. One is to set a timer and stick as close to 10 to 15 minutes as possible. The other is to avoid asking questions to the whole group. For example, asking the question, "Who remembers what we learned yesterday about how characters in stories can change over time?" may lead to multiple unfocused answers that unnecessarily extend time. Instead, start by rephrasing this to, "Learners, yesterday we learned about how characters in stories can change over time. They may start out one way, but as the story evolves, they change, and they are different by the end."

How much student conversation should happen during the mini-lesson?

Students may be asked to speak with a partner during the active engagement part of the mini-lesson. Give students roughly one to three minutes to hold their conversations, depending on the task involved. Keep in mind that all students, but especially English learners, will benefit from sentence starters or frames as well as wait time.

QSSSA (Q Triple-S A), which stands for **Question, Signal, Stem, Share, Assess**, is an instructional method that fits in nicely here to support English learners and all students with effective talk during the mini-lesson (Seidlitz & Perryman, 2011). It is not an addition to the mini-lesson and does not lengthen the mini-lesson. Rather, it enhances the mini-lesson by adding a scaffold for powerful discussion.

Q-S-S-S-A

Q-Question: Pose an open-ended, engaging question.

S-Signal: Ask student to show a signal when they are prepared to answer the question.

S-Stem: Provide a sentence frame or starter.

S-Share: Students share with a partner or group.

A-Assess: Randomly select a few students to share with the whole group.

Supporting English Learners at Various English Proficiency Levels in Mini-Lessons

ENTERING	EMERGING	DEVELOPING/ EXPANDING	BRIDGING/ REACHING
1	2	3	4/5
Beginning	Intermediate	Advanced	Advanced High
• Provide simple sentence stems • Place student in a triad with a same-langue-speaking peer and an English speaking peer • Preview content in primary language • Allow primary language support • Use extensive visuals, illustration, gestures, realia • Use slower speech • Respect the silent period	• Provide simple sentence stems • Provide a word bank with visuals and/or primary language support • Use visuals, illustrations, gestures, realia • Use slower speech • Allow ample wait time	• Provide complex sentence stems • Use some visuals and gestures • Allow ample wait time	• Provide complex sentence stems • Use some visuals and gestures • Allow ample wait time

Should I expect all of my students to master what I've taught during the mini-lesson?

No, your mini-lesson is not the only time students will have the opportunity to hear or practice this skill. We can't expect students to master the skill in the 10 to 15 minutes that we present it. Don't worry if they don't. This is just an introduction.

Do I need separate mini-lessons for reading and writing?

The answer to this varies depending on how the language arts block of time is structured at your school or district. In some cases, reading and writing are completely integrated into one subject. They could be taught together in one mini-lesson. However, if reading and writing are taught separately, then two different mini-lessons would be appropriate.

Will I teach a mini-lesson every day?

Yes, mini-lessons are taught daily. We suggest planning mini-lessons for Monday through Thursday, leaving Friday free for addressing skills and concepts that come up during the week.

How much time should I spend planning the mini-lesson?

Since the mini-lesson is a small portion of daily reading and writing instruction, planning for it does not require a great amount of time. This frees us up for planning our small-group instruction and supporting students at more individualized levels.

Chapter 3

Read-Aloud

> "**Read-Aloud** is a way to honor students' culture and interests, as well as build background and vocabulary."
>
> — Regie Routman

WHAT IS A READ-ALOUD?

Fewer things are more enjoyable to teachers and students alike than a read-aloud. Reading aloud to a classroom community is one of the most fundamental tasks we can do with our students. Through reading aloud, we are able to build students' listening, speaking, reading, and writing skills, and more. In a typical classroom read-aloud, the teacher reads a text to students while stopping occasionally and purposefully to do a "think-aloud" or to allow students to negotiate for meaning. During a read-aloud, it is not necessary to provide students with a copy of the text; however, doing so can be beneficial to English learners as they build language and literacy. It is also highly beneficial to share illustrations with students while reading aloud.

Reading aloud to students provides them with an explicit model of real, authentic reading from one who is more proficient than they are. Read-alouds are part of the I DO in the Gradual Release of Responsibility model coined by Pearson and Gallagher (1983). They can come in many forms, as teachers can read from big books, picture books, chapter books, nonfiction, poetry, brochures, etc.

One of the main purposes of reading aloud is for students to experience hearing the reading and thinking of a proficient reader. What does the reader sound like? What does the reader think and do? We want our readers to comprehend what they choose to listen to and read on their own.

Through read-alouds, we are able to scaffold their comprehension. Comprehending texts is the ultimate goal of reading. Yet students struggle with comprehension when they lack fluency and an understanding of key vocabulary. Reading aloud to students gives us opportunities to model both of these and more (Tompkins, 2015). ELs especially need to hear what English language structures sound like frequently, including the appropriate speed and intonation and prosody. Without these elements of reading, written language is difficult to comprehend.

I remember several years ago when I was strengthening my reading skills in Serbian, my mother sent me an email that was a paragraph long (about six sentences). It took me nearly an hour to decode the paragraph. By the time I finished, I had a terrible headache and I had no idea what I'd read. Something very similar happens with our English learners who are not yet proficient in English. When they are reading or being read to, they must devote part of their attention to the language and part to the academic content.

—Valentina

The explicit instruction and modeling in a read-aloud prepares students to be successful on their own. Reading aloud sets a foundation for independence by equipping students with the skills they need to achieve reading success. Independence is not achieved all at once, but over time with support that is reduced as necessary.

Gradual Release of Responsibility & Components of Literacy

I do	We do	You do
• Mini-Lesson	• Shared Reading	• Independent Reading
★ Read-Aloud	• Guided Reading	• Independent Writing
• Write-Aloud	• Shared Writing	

| explicit & modeled | structured & supported | automatic & natural |

WHAT A READ-ALOUD IS NOT

Sometimes the term "read-aloud" is confused with the act of calling on students randomly to read sections or sentences from a text (also known as round-robin or popcorn reading). This variation of reading is sometimes seen in classrooms in an effort to engage students and keep participation up. However, it can actually do more harm than good to readers. Think back to your own experiences with this as a young reader in school. Those of us who struggled with reading or were embarrassed by speaking in front of our peers may recall the stress round-robin created. As readers are waiting to be called on, anxiety rises and comprehension declines. According to Donalyn Miller (2009), "Round-robin reading does nothing to foster a feeling of reading success in any but the best readers, and it doesn't

build anyone's oral reading ability or fluency, either" (p. 147). Not to mention, English learners who are struggling to keep up with both language and content now must also keep anxiety in check.

Read-aloud is also not the basic act of reading a text out loud to the class. Though the term "read-aloud" seems to indicate that one would be simply reading aloud, in order for the method to be accessible to all students, think-aloud and embedded discourse are necessary.

Read-aloud is not asking students to read their own copies of a text aloud. Though this technique is helpful for some students as they read, read-aloud itself uses the teacher as the model.

the Benefits OF Reading Aloud TO English Learners

Gonzalez, 2016

@ValentinaESL

- expand language structures

- relax minds & reduce stress

- highlight culture & interests

- grow vocabulary

- inspire writers

- inspire readers

- bond & build community

- create background knowledge

- strengthen comprehension

- explore various genres

- grow grammar

THE BENEFITS OF READING ALOUD TO ENGLISH LEARNERS

Beyond drawing all students into a text and demonstrating fluent reading, read-alouds are multifaceted in their benefits. Much like our iPhones these days (which we use for more than just phone calls) read-alouds can accomplish multiple instructional goals.

Even though reading aloud to students is immensely powerful, it is often one of the first instructional practices that gets removed from the lesson plans when time runs out. Due to the pressures of curriculum and grading, and because reading aloud to students is not graded, typically this critical piece of the puzzle gets left out. Unfortunately when this happens, students and schools pay for it in the long run. Because reading aloud is foundational, when we remove it from the equation, many students are left with listening, speaking, reading, and writing gaps that show through in state and local testing. In his article, "Read Aloud Often and Well," Lester Laminack (2017) says that reading aloud to students paves the way for and is an investment in future work.

At a conference once, a teacher came to me and thanked me for sharing information on the power of reading aloud to students. He said he felt validated for the work he was doing. Reading aloud to English learners may be the only time they hear a proficient model of reading in English. The benefits of reading aloud to students outweigh the reasons not to read aloud to them.

— Valentina

ACCOMMODATING READ-ALOUD FOR ENGLISH LEARNERS

For English learners, a read-aloud can be a point of struggle. Simply reading text to students may not be comprehensible. To make read-aloud more accessible for all students, but especially for English learners, we can employ specific techniques that maximize this instructional method.

Interactive read-alouds create spaces for students to stop and think about the reading, talk with a partner, act out a scene, draw, or write. We can set students up for success by explicitly modeling expectations. Take, for example, this lesson below.

The teacher has pulled the class up to the reading rug and is reading a book called *The Empty Pot* (Demi, 1990). Students are seated by predetermined language partners.

Teacher: *We have read so far that Ping's seed is not growing. Soon all the children will take their pots to the Emperor, and he will choose a successor. What do you think Ping should do?*

The teacher writes on chart paper:
"Partner A: I think Ping should… because…"
"Partner B: I agree/disagree because…"

Techniques to make read-alouds more comprehensible:

- Including opportunities for peer-to-peer interaction
- Embedding "Stop and Draw (or Write)"
- Using gestures and visuals
- Enunciating and speaking slowly

Teacher: *Let's read these together.*

The teacher leads students in chorally reading the sentence stems. This provides students with the language structures and support to complete their own thoughts. Then, the teacher points to the sentence stems.

Teacher: *When you can complete this sentence, put your hand on your head.*

When all students are ready, the teacher continues. This provides students with think time.

Teacher: *Partner A will share first. Partner B, listen and decide if you agree or disagree and why. When you are finished sharing together, put your hands on your knees so I can see that you are ready to read on.*

Creating a more interactive experience for learners allows students to achieve the following:

• Think more critically about the text
• Negotiate for meaning using vocabulary related to the text
• Increase participation and engagement
• Listen to a peer's point of view
• Build on their own ideas or a peer's idea

Another way to support ELs with read-alouds is to provide multiple readings of the text. This can be done in a few different ways. One is through pre-reading. For students who need extra support with grammar and vocabulary, pre-reading the text with them in a small group will give them time to hear the text before they experience it with the larger group. You can take advantage of this time with the small group to cover **vocabulary** and misconceptions.

You may also consider providing some students with an audio version of the text to listen to at their leisure. Students can listen and follow along with the printed copy of the text at home. If this is available, it is highly effective for language learners.

One more way to get in multiple readings is to reread the text with a small group of students while the remainder of the class is independently reading. In the small group, the students can participate in a shared reading (either echo reading, choral reading, or a Reader's Theater style). If you have the benefit of a co-teacher in your room, take advantage of this and have the co-teacher reread the text with students, stopping now and then to discuss key points and critical vocabulary.

POWerful Interactive READ-ALOUDS
• provide think time
• allow turn & talk
• stop to write or draw
• act out

Supporting English Learners in Read-Alouds

Possible EL Struggles	Suggestions to Support ELs
Too much oral input	Use visuals, picture books
Difficult vocabulary	Pre-teach critical vocabulary
Lack of opportunities to talk	Embed opportunities for student-to-student interaction
As ELs get older, read-alouds get fewer	Read aloud to all ages/grades
Fictional text is culturally biased	Provide a healthy balance of genres
ELs feel underrepresented in texts	Provide culturally inclusive texts

CLASSROOM SCENARIO

Think back to the three classrooms highlighted in this book. Remember Ms. Montrose and her first graders? Here's what a typical read-aloud may look like in Ms. Montrose's classroom to support the needs of the English learners at various proficiency levels.

Ms. Montrose looked at her first grade reading standards and has decided that the overall goal will be for students to follow a plot with multiple events and notice and understand when a problem is solved. She has selected a picture book called *Alma and How She Got Her Name*, written by Juana Martinez-Neal (2018). Her decision to read this book was also based on her classroom dynamics. The class has many students with unique names, and she feels that this book will empower students to feel comfortable with them.

As Ms. Montrose pre-read the book, she took note of five vocabulary words that students would need to know ahead of the read-aloud: jasmine, sailor, plazas, ancestors, and charm. Ms. Montrose decided to provide visuals for these words, so she gathered a few images to share with students before reading the book. In addition to looking for vocabulary, Ms. Montrose decided on specific places to stop and think aloud. She placed several sticky notes throughout the text to remind her of what she wanted to say to the students. Ms. Montrose also planned intentional stopping points for students to interact with one another.

To introduce the book, Ms. Montrose gave a book talk about why she had carefully chosen this book to read to the class and how important our names are to each of us.

Ms. Montrose: *Boys and girls, I am so excited about the book we are going to share today! It's one of my favorites. It's called Alma and How She Got Her Name. I picked this book for you all today because I know how special your names are to you. All of our names are unique and special. Someone carefully picked your name just like I carefully picked out this book for us today. Before we find out how Alma got her name, I want to share with you a few words from the book. One word that we're going to read in this book is "jasmine." Jasmine is a type of plant that has a white flower. It looks like this, and it has a fragrant smell like perfume.*

Ms. Montrose shows an image under the document camera and labels it "jasmine, plant, white flower, fragrant smell." She points out the cognate for jasmine in Spanish, jazmín. Ms. Montrose continues to share the other vocabulary words in the same way.

Ms. Montrose reads the book aloud to the class as they sit in close proximity. She remembers to speak clearly and at an easy pace. Occasionally, she uses gestures to support understanding.

While reading, she stops to think aloud and to provide opportunities for students to turn and talk with their partners using sentence frames. Ms. Montrose sets students up for success by modeling the expectations for student talk.

Ms. Montrose: *Partners, let's talk about the characters we've met so far and what we've learned. Turn and face your partner. Partner A will talk first, then Partner B. Remember that each of you will share. Let's all say this together. "One character from the story is... I learned that..."*

Letty and Victoria are partners. Let's take a look at what they say to each other.

Letty: *One character from the story was José. I learned that José was an artist like me.*

Victoria: *One character from the story was Sofia. I learned that Sofia loved books.*

Ms. Montrose calls on a few students by drawing their popsicle sticks to share what they talked about with their partners. Then she begins to read again and stops for a think-aloud.

Ms. Montrose: *The author, Juana, just gave me a lot of information. I need to stop and think about it. So Sofia was the name of Alma's grandmother, and she also loved books and flowers. Just like Alma!*

Ms. Montrose continues to read, stop to think aloud, and give partners topics to discuss with sentence stems.

Following the read-aloud, students are asked to write in their journals. Ms. Montrose scaffolds student writing with the previous talk opportunities about the events in the story and the problem and solution. When students return to their work areas, they write about the problem and how it was solved. They use the following sentence stems:

The problem was... It was solved when...
At the beginning of the story, Alma's problem was... because...
At the end of the story, the problem was solved when... because...

Some students draw, others write in sentences, and some use their primary language.

WHAT THE EXPERTS SAY

In *The Read-Aloud Handbook,* author and researcher Jim Trelease (2013) writes that "the best way to accumulate background knowledge is by either reading or being read to" (p. 14). In addition, he suggests that as we read to children, we are providing sounds, syllables, endings, and blends that the children will someday read on their own.

Reading aloud to students is "an excellent opportunity for students to discuss high-quality fiction, nonfiction, and poetry" (Fountas & Pinnell, 2001, p. 29).

Serafini (2015) states that "there is no instructional approach that is more effective or efficient than reading aloud with children" (p. 34). He goes on to explain that the act of reading aloud is not something we do to students; rather "we read along with them" (p. 34). Students engage by participating in listening, questioning, and discussing with partners.

Read-Aloud Lesson Map

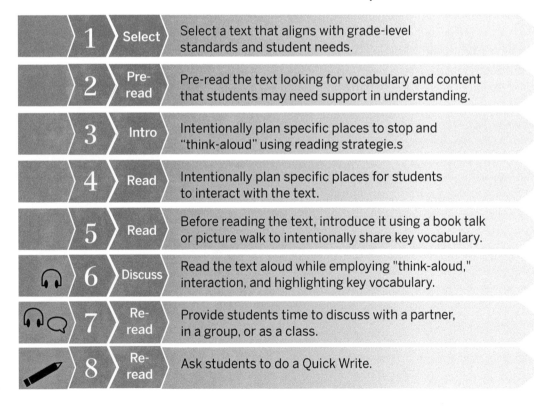

1	Select	Select a text that aligns with grade-level standards and student needs.
2	Pre-read	Pre-read the text looking for vocabulary and content that students may need support in understanding.
3	Intro	Intentionally plan specific places to stop and "think-aloud" using reading strategie.s
4	Read	Intentionally plan specific places for students to interact with the text.
5	Read	Before reading the text, introduce it using a book talk or picture walk to intentionally share key vocabulary.
6	Discuss	Read the text aloud while employing "think-aloud," interaction, and highlighting key vocabulary.
7	Re-read	Provide students time to discuss with a partner, in a group, or as a class.
8	Re-read	Ask students to do a Quick Write.

FAQ

How do I choose a text to read aloud to my students?

Begin by looking at the content standards and determine what students need to know. Next, find a text that meets the standard and is compelling and relevant to the students you work with. The text can come in many forms. It may be a picture book, but it could also be a chapter from a larger book, a short story, a paragraph, a poem, a brochure, or a newspaper article.

How long should my read-alouds be?

A typical read-aloud is about 10 to 15 minutes, but that can be flexible. Some teachers find that creating a sacred space and time for daily read-alouds not only builds a routine for students but also ensures that read-alouds are not scrapped. A typical read-aloud sequence begins with a short teacher introduction, the reading of the text with embedded teacher think-alouds and opportunities for student-to-student talk, and finally ends with a whole-group or small-group conversation to wrap up the read-aloud. Other teachers have included a Quick Write (three-minute writing) after students have had an opportunity to discuss with their peers. (See the Read-Aloud Lesson Map for more details). One great way to keep the read-aloud experiences always at the forefront of learning and keep an ongoing record of reading is to make a class list of the texts that have been shared.

How often should I stop to think aloud or let students talk with a partner?

Planning when to stop and think aloud or let students talk with a partner is best when it's done ahead of time. Intentionally planning questions and sentence stems ensures that academic language is planted into the

Reading aloud to students is planting seeds... seeds of vocabulary, language structures, writing, grammar, & independent reading. @ValentinaESL

Supporting English Learners at Various English Proficiency Levels in Read-Alouds

WIDA
ELPA 21
ELPS/TELPAS

ENTERING	EMERGING	DEVELOPING/ EXPANDING	BRIDGING/ REACHING
1	2	3	4/5
Beginning	Intermediate	Advanced	Advanced High
• Provide simple sentence stems	• Provide simple sentence stems	• Provide complex sentence stems	• Provide complex sentence stems
• Place student in a triad with a same-languge-speaking peer and an English speaking peer	• Provide a word bank with visuals and/or primary language support	• Use some visuals and gestures	• Use some visuals and gestures
• Preview content in primary language	• Use visuals, illustrations, gesture, realia	• Allow ample wait time	• Allow ample wait time
• Allow primary language support	• Use slower speech		
• Use extensive visuals, illustration, gestures, realia	• Allow ample wait time		
• Use slower speech			
• Chunk reading into small sections			
• Respect the silent period			

conversation. The days before you read the text to students, pre-read it to yourself and spy on yourself as a reader. Think about what you do as a reader. Write sticky notes, and purposefully plan places in the text where you will talk through your thinking. Then gradually release and allow dedicated time for the students to do the thinking as they participate in structured conversations with partners, such as with a strategy like QSSSA (see p. 34 for more information).

Keep in mind that there's no need to stop to do a think-aloud or let students talk on every page. In fact, that may make the reading and comprehension choppy. Consider the flow of the text and comprehension when planning stopping points (Gallagher, 2009).

My students struggle with connecting to the texts. What can I do?

Carefully considering text selections based on students and their cultures is key to engagement. Take inventory of your classroom. Who are your students? What are their backgrounds? What are their passions? When selecting read-alouds, vary the options. When students see themselves in the texts we present, they feel validated and represented. In addition to reading aloud narrative texts, we can also read aloud expository texts. Providing a balance of various genres helps all students find connections. A healthy balance of genres in read-alouds is key.

How do I support students who are at the beginner or entering level of language proficiency in English?

Prior to the read-aloud, preview the text selection, and pay close attention to vocabulary and concepts that newcomer students may need additional support with. Look for cultural barriers that may create misunderstandings, and provide students with scaffolds such as visuals, realia, or primary language previews before the read-aloud begins. Students who have little English proficiency will benefit from exposure to key vocabulary words prior to the read-aloud. When possible, gather students in a small group and preview three to nine main words from the reading. Introduce these words using visuals and primary language support.

Are my students too old for a read-aloud?

Students are never too old to be read aloud to. Often students' listening and cognitive levels are higher than their reading and speaking levels (Sticht & James, 1984). Routman (2005) states, "...reading aloud is a necessity for developing language that students cannot yet read on their own" (p. 124). When students are not read aloud to, they are not given the opportunity to hear text at the level they may be able to comprehend. This can create gaps in learning. Reading aloud to students of all ages helps them continue hearing proficient reading at higher levels than they can decode on their own. This allows students to receive input on language structures, grammar, and vocabulary that they may not hear or read if they were not read aloud to.

What do I do with texts that I've already read-aloud to my students?

There are many options. One way to use these texts is with small groups of students as shared readings. Since students have heard the text from you as a model of reading, thinking, and fluency, this scaffold will help them as they move through the Gradual Release of Responsibility model to the WE DO phase (Pearson & Gallagher, 1983). In the shared reading, students can either echo read or choral read with you (see p.115 & 116). This continues to offer accommodations for Beginning, Entering, and Emerging English learners.

Another option is to create Reader's Theater style readings with the text (Young & Rasinski, 2009). Some texts lend themselves naturally to this technique. It doesn't have to be anything elaborate, simply selecting designated sections for each group to read aloud chorally will do. Allowing groups some rehearsal time beforehand will lower the affective filter and prepare all students for the reading presentation.

My administrators don't see the value in read-alouds. What do I do?

It's important that the school has a common belief and vision for language and literacy. If we value reading and language, then we should be able to quantify the value in our lesson plans and daily instruction. Share with administrators why reading aloud benefits your students. Reading aloud to students is the first step in the Gradual Release of Responsibility Model. If we want students to read, write, speak, and listen using high academic vocabulary, reading aloud sets the stage. In Laura Varlas' (2018) article, "Why Every Class Needs Read Aloud," Regie Routman suggests inviting an administrator in during read-aloud "so they can listen to the level of conversation that takes place and see how engaged kids are."

I have a heterogenous class of students who are all at different language levels. How do I accommodate a read-aloud to meet everyone's needs?

Most classrooms are heterogenous, with students at all different levels of proficiency in language, regardless of whether they are identified as English learners or not. There are many ways to vary the instruction of your read-aloud so that all learners benefit and grow. The chart on p. 47, "Supporting English Learners at Various English Proficiency Levels in ReadAlouds," will give you some ideas to target specific English language proficiency levels and intentionally plan for progress.

In one of my second grade classes, I had several English learners. When I read aloud to my students, I sat in a rocking chair while my students sat on the floor to hear the story. A few students, including some of the English learners, stood beside my chair, sometimes even perching on the arms of the chair to get as close to the book as they could. As I introduced the book, they touched the pictures and asked questions about the pictures and the words. We discussed the vocabulary and talked about how our own experiences related to the words we were reading. As I read, students naturally asked questions and we looked for answers in the text. The students standing around me continued to touch the book and talk about the pictures and the story. Some of them actually even wanted to be inside the book.

Many times, they would write about what they had read during a read-aloud and would draw pictures. We also frequently acted out the stories in groups after the readings, using language from the text. I remember what a meaningful experience that was for all of us. My English learners benefited from our discussions about vocabulary, their conversations with their peers, and with me about the book. With this support, my students were able to comprehend the text while learning new vocabulary and listening to fluent reading.

– Melinda

Chapter 4

Shared Reading

> "There's so much more to a *book* than just the reading."
> – Maurice Sendak

WHAT IS SHARED READING?

Shared reading is a method of involving the whole class in reading a text together. In shared reading, everyone has access to the same text, which they read together as the teacher leads the way. Typically, the text is read repeatedly over multiple days, focusing on various teaching points.

In primary classrooms, shared reading may come in the form of a big book that the teacher displays in front of students as they gather at a common reading area. Teachers may focus more on print, letter sound, and the foundations of reading.

Shared reading in upper elementary classrooms may look slightly different. The teacher may display a text under a document camera for all to see, or each student could have a copy of the text. Teachers may then focus on closer analysis of this text.

I was reminded of the effectiveness of shared reading while attending a holiday concert where the choir director led us in what I considered to be a variation of shared reading of the song he was singing. Picture this: The words were scrolling on the big screen for us all to see. As he was singing, each word was highlighted. He encouraged us to join in by shouting, "Come on, now!" and beckoning us with his arms. As we joined, he pointed the mic at us. Occasionally, when a new and more challenging part was coming up, he said, "The next line goes like this..." and he modeled it for us before it came on the screen. This was his way of employing echo reading (See p. 115). He led the way by example, his expressions and tone helping us to know better how to sing each additional verse.

—*Valentina*

Shared reading provides an opportunity for all students to put their eyes on the same text and practice reading together under the careful supervision and guidance of the teacher. The guided instruction and modeling provided by the teacher in shared reading supports students to be successful on their own.

Shared reading is used as a vehicle of instruction. We need students to gain certain reading and thinking practices or goals, such as learning phonics using authentic text or learning to make predictions. Shared reading helps us get them there by ensuring that they actively participate in reading, speaking, and thinking using a text that is slightly higher than their instructional level. When ELs at beginning and intermediate levels of proficiency are provided with sufficient background information, shared reading can even be a significant source of comprehensible input.

WHAT SHARED READING IS NOT

Though shared reading is often seen in the younger grades, it is not only for primary classrooms. Even students in grades three and up benefit from shared reading. In older grades, shared reading may not look the same, but the value is still as great. Older students still need to practice reading on grade level in a safe environment in which they are free to take risks. Thus, shared reading opens a space for low-risk reading that includes every kind of learner in the classroom.

Shared reading can be used for more than just fiction. In fact, bringing in biographies, poetry, comics, daily news, captions, how-to instructions, and other materials that are engaging and relevant to students will greatly enhance their reading pleasure and stretch their vocabularies. Shared reading can be done with shorter readings or more lengthy pieces.

Gradual Release of Responsibility & Components of Literacy

I do	We do	You do
• Mini-Lesson	★ Shared Reading	• Independent Reading
• Read-Aloud	• Guided Reading	• Independent Writing
• Write-Aloud	• Shared Writing	

explicit & modeled	structured & supported	automatic & natural

There is a misconception that shared reading is only for whole-group instruction. This is not the case. Shared reading can be implemented in small groups, too. Many students benefit from a smaller, more intimate setting, and the lower student-teacher ratio can support students who need more tailored interventions. Some English learners at lower proficiency levels may gain more from shared reading in small groups than they would with the whole class.

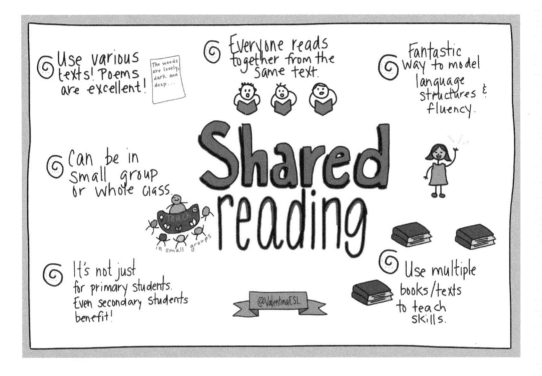

THE BENEFITS OF SHARED READING FOR ENGLISH LEARNERS

Shared reading can support students by providing a nice foundation for the way letters, sounds, and words work together. All students can benefit from the shared reading experience, but English learners especially make great gains from the structure of reading together as a group.

Shared reading is an opportunity to directly teach intonation, language structures, and fluency. Author Kylene Beers (2003) says, "It's one thing to model fluent reading and another to directly teach students how to use correct phrasing and intonation" (p. 216).

Shared Reading benefits English learners because it accomplishes many things:

• Lowers the affective filter and provides a safe space

• Builds a sense of success

• Strengthens fluency

• Develops thinking and reading processes

• Models prosody and English language structures

• Fosters a sense of community

ACCOMMODATING SHARED READING FOR ENGLISH LEARNERS

Shared reading supports readers of all kinds. It helps students feel that they are part of the reading community. When English learners need additional support with shared reading, you can try several tactics:

• Providing the text in the students' primary language for preview
• Using primary language supports such as translation dictionaries
• Providing opportunities for peer discussion
• Offering sentence frames for structured conversations
• Using gestures and visuals
• Tracking text and pointing to words and visuals

CLASSROOM SCENARIO

Mr. Menil's third grade students are very excited about shared reading. They enjoy reading together as a class, and Mr. Menil makes this experience enjoyable for them. He begins with a quick introduction of the book. This time, he has selected *The Day You Begin* by Jacqueline Woodson because he has a new student and wants to build empathy and create a comfortable environment. After the introduction, Mr. Menil projects the book under a document camera and invites students to discuss with one another.

Mr. Menil: *Think of a time when you felt different. Share with you partner, using the sentence stem, "I felt different when..."*

Students share in pairs. Jennifer and Manuel are partners. Let's take a look at what they say to each other.

Jennifer: *I felt different when I had a big bow in my hair and nobody else had a bow. I felt like a baby.*

Manuel: *I felt different when my grandma came to open house and she was speaking Spanish to me. She only speaks Spanish.*

Jennifer: *That's cool! I wish I could speak Spanish!*

Mr. Menil reads the book to the class as they listen. Every now and then, he stops to think aloud.

Mr. Menil: *I'm wondering how the character is feeling right here.*

Following the first read, Mr. Menil leads the class in another quick discussion.

Mr. Menil: *There are times when I've felt different, too. The other day, I had lunch with my friends, and everyone else had sandwiches, but I had brought saag paneer. I felt like everyone was staring at my food. So I offered for my friends to try my food. What can you do when you feel different?*

Manuel: *You can go stand by somebody and talk to them, or you can offer to share your food with them like you did.*

Mr. Menil: *Ah, that's a good idea, Manuel. It always makes you feel better when you talk to somebody and connect with them, right?*

After discussion, Mr. Menil invites the class to read the story with him. This is a practice they are familiar with. However, if students are new to shared reading, teachers may need to coach the class on how to read in unison.

Mr. Menil is careful not to slow down too much during the reading. He wants the flow and fluency of the reading to be natural for students to mimic. Some students can be heard reading loudly and prominently while others whisper or take breaks to listen in on more proficient readers.

On subsequent days, Mr. Menil and his class reread the book and address new learning goals such as the following:
• Word work
• Vocabulary
• Punctuation
• Writer's craft

After four to five rereadings, the book is made available to all readers for independent reading. Now all students are able to read this book successfully on their own.

Broadly speaking, language can only 'grow' through interaction with people and texts that introduce new vocabulary, concepts, and language structures.

WHAT THE EXPERTS SAY

The National Reading Panel (2000) found that, "repeated reading and other procedures that have students reading passages orally multiple times while receiving guidance or feedback from peers, parents, or teachers are effective in improving a variety of reading skills" (p. 208). The NRP also found that these same procedures helped improve students' reading ability, at least through grade five, and proved successful for students with learning problems much later than this. In addition, the NRP found that "repeated reading and other guided oral reading procedures have clearly been shown to improve fluency

and overall reading achievement" (p. 216). If students only experience text on their own independent level of reading, then gaps in education will continue to expand. English learners' listening comprehension is likely to be at higher levels than their reading comprehension. By providing them opportunities to hear text at higher cognitive levels, we allow them opportunities to think, negotiate for meaning, and grapple with ideas at levels they aren't exposed to in their independent reading. Biemiller (2003) emphasizes that young learners' listening comprehension progresses and builds through elementary school. Naturally, students in earlier grade levels comprehend less than students in more advanced grade levels. "Broadly speaking, language can only 'grow' through interaction with people and texts that introduce new vocabulary, concepts, and language structures." Biemiller argues that it is necessary for students to experience language growth through means other than independent reading because "most children are not reading content that is as advanced as their oral language."

Shared Reading Lesson Map

1	Select	Select a text that aligns with the grade level standards and learning goals.
2	Pre-read	Pre-read the text looking for vocabulary and content that students may need support in understanding.
3	Intro	Before sharing the text aloud, give a brief introduction.
4	Read	Project the text and model reading it aloud to the class, followed by a brief discussion.
5	Read	Read the text together as a class.
6	Discuss	Invite student to discuss the meaning of the text.
7	Re-read	Revisit the text on subsequent days and reread it, focusing on specific teaching points.

FAQ

How do I choose a text for shared reading?

Begin by deciding on learning goals for your class. These will be identified by looking at grade-appropriate state standards and then selecting texts that will be engaging vehicles for these goals. Compelling and relevant texts are most likely to grab and hold the attention of students. Culturally inclusive texts draw students and their background knowledge in to instruction. Using texts that students connect with will enrich shared reading while validating students' identities. Shared reading is a perfect opportunity to build classroom community and foster empathy.

How long should shared readings take?

The length of shared reading varies based on your learning goals and the text you select. Start with the end in mind. What is it that students need to know and be able to do by the end of the lesson? Look at grade level and age appropriate goals and standards. Next, select a text that will be a vehicle for the goals. Texts for shared reading range from excerpts to picture books to Reader's Theater. These can take 20 to 45 minutes to read and discuss each day, and span over four to five days.

What do I do with a text we used as a shared reading?

After a text has been shared as a shared reading, make it available to all students to use during independent reading. Thanks to the scaffolding provided by repeated shared readings of the text, students are prepared to read and understand this text independently.

Students can also use shared reading as a model for writing. They can use the text as an example and write a similar piece. For instance, a primary class may read *The Very Hungry Caterpillar* and then write their own version (Carle, 2014). Students may write about The Very ___ ___ (The Very Happy Bear or The Very Sad Kitten, etc). The teacher can support students with sentence stems, frames, and visuals.

Graphic adapted from content in Bishop, 1990

One year, I read the big book, *A House is a House for Me* with my second graders as a shared reading. We read it several times and talked about the houses different animals live in. The students then rewrote the book, with each child providing a page on which they finished the sentence stem, "A _____ is a house for a _____." They came up with clever texts such as "You are a house for your heart," and "A domino is a house for some dots."

— *Melinda*

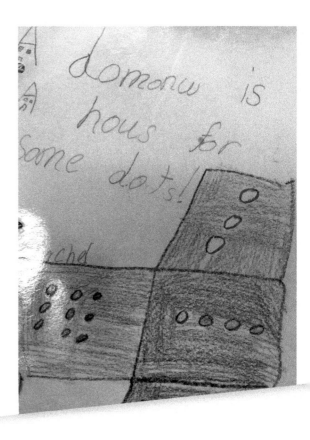

Another option for writing is to have students reflect by responding to the text. What surprised them? What did the text remind them of? How did the text make them feel? Sentence stems or frames may support English learners with language structures for developing their writing.

The book called ____ reminded me of the time when...because...

We read the book called___. What surprised me most was when...It surprised me because...This made me feel...

How do I support students who are emergent readers in English?

One way to support students who are emergent readers is to label the classroom together. When labeling the room, we can allow student input and sometimes use students' native languages as we identify and name various objects. This can be an excellent way to build readers' self-esteem and value students' other languages. The labels can be used for reading practice during transition times. Some teachers even create fun games to play with students using the labeled words. Imagine if after the first day of pre-K or kindergarten, you went home feeling like you were a reader!

How do I support students who are at the beginner or entering level of language proficiency in English?

Shared reading is an important component of language development for English learners, but students at earlier levels of proficiency will need extra support. One way to give extra support is through echo reading. The teacher simply reads a line or page and asks students to repeat after him or her. Students hear the teacher and mimic what and how the teacher reads. For example:

> **Teacher:** Class, today I will read a page, and then I want you to read after me. I want you to be my echo. I'll read, and then you read the same words. Try to sound like me. Let's try it. "There will be times when you walk into a room and no one there is quite like you."

> **Students:** There will be times when you walk into a room and no one there is quite like you.

Another way to accommodate shared reading for English learners is to do this during small-group instruction rather than with the whole group. By providing shared reading in small groups, you can more directly meet the specific needs of English learners at earlier English proficiency levels. Students at early proficiency levels may need different learning goals or different texts, and they may gain more from discussions (using sentence frames) in a smaller setting under the more careful eyes and ears of the teacher.

Harnessing the power of students' primary language during shared reading can support English learners at earlier proficiency levels. If the shared reading text is available in students' primary language, provide it to them prior to reading it in English. When available, allow students the opportunity to talk about the reading with a same-language-speaking peer in their primary language. These practices allow for translanguaging and enable students to view language repertoires as a source of strength rather than a deficit (Ascenzi-Moreno, 2018).

Are my students too old for shared reading?

For students in their earlier years of classroom instruction, Fountas and Pinnell (2017) tell us that "shared reading plays a vital role in helping students understand how to find and use information from print—directional movement, one-to-one correspondence, words and letters, and the whole act of reading and understanding a story or nonfiction text." Then, as these learners become more proficient readers, the process of shared reading "continues to offer opportunities for more advanced reading work than students can do independently" (p. 85).

I have a heterogenous class of students that are all at different language levels. How do I accommodate my shared reading to meet everyone's needs?

It is not uncommon to have a class that is heterogenous and to worry about how your shared reading will meet everyone's needs. Selecting texts that are above students' independent reading levels is important. Since shared reading is heavily supported by the teacher, students are able to listen to and mimic the teacher as he or she models the reading process and thinking that goes into reading the text.

The chart below will give you some ideas to target specific English language proficiency levels and intentionally plan for progress.

Supporting English Learners at Various English Proficiency Levels in Shared Reading

WIDA
ELPA 21
ELPS/TELPAS

ENTERING	EMERGING	DEVELOPING/ EXPANDING	BRIDGING/ REACHING
1	2	3	4/5
Beginning	Intermediate	Advanced	Advanced High
• Provide simple sentence stems for opportunities to talk • Place student in a triad with a same-languge-speaking peer and an English speaking peer • Preview content in primary language • Allow primary language support • Use extensive visuals, illustration, gestures, realia • Employ echo reading • Gather students in small groups • Select culturally inclusive words	• Provide simple sentence stems for opportunities to talk • Use visuals, illustrations, gestures, realia • Employ echo reading • Gather students in small groups • Select culturally inclusive words	• Provide complex sentence stems for opportunities to talk • Use visuals and gestures as needed • Allow ample wait time • Select culturally inclusive words	• Provide complex sentence stems for opportunities to talk • Use visuals and gestures as needed • Allow ample wait time • Select culturally inclusive words

I recently worked with a group of fourth and fifth grade English learners in an after-school program. They had each independently read the book *Touching Spirit Bear* by Ben Mikaelsen (2001). This was a high-interest book for the students, and they were motivated to read it because it is about a boy close to their age who goes through many struggles. I chose to do a shared reading with the group in the form of Reader's Theater. I wrote a script for them based on a portion of the text, and I passed out the script to the students. We first read over the script as a shared reading, then we talked about unfamiliar or tricky words, and I provided a simple explanation of each. Then the students chose parts, and I guided them through several minutes of practice. I noticed that the students put a lot of expression and feeling into their reading, and they became more and more fluent as they read. They were supportive of each other and helped one another with pronunciation and phrasing. I could tell they all wanted to do a good job on the script.

Next, the students performed the script for the rest of the class in the after-school program. The next time I met with them, the students created their own Reader's Theater script from another section of the book. After they wrote the script together, we read it together as a shared reading, and then they chose parts and practiced for several minutes. The students each took home the script to practice. In a few weeks, the author, Ben Mikaelsen, visited the students, and they performed the Reader's Theater script they wrote for him. The students did an excellent job with the scripts and read fluently and with expression. The smiles on their faces as Ben Mikaelsen complimented them on their performances said it all!

— Melinda

Chapter 5

Guided Reading

"**Reading** is breathing in, and **writing** is breathing out."

— Pam Allyn

The previous two chapters both focused on ways teachers can provide direct support for their students. Now let's look at how we can use the next phase, guided reading, to move our students into reading on their own. As the name implies, guided reading still includes teacher guidance, but as students participate in the reading of novel texts, they begin to develop strategies that will enable them to read more independently.

WHAT IS GUIDED READING?

In guided reading, the teacher meets with a small group of students at similar reading levels. The teacher begins by introducing the book and then having the students read the book aloud simultaneously but not in unison as if it were a choral read. As students read, the teacher listens in on individual students and prompts them when they get to an

Gradual Release of Responsibility & Components of Literacy

I do — **We do** — **You do**

- Mini-Lesson
- Read-Aloud
- Write-Aloud

- Shared Reading
- ★ Guided Reading
- Shared Writing

- Independent Reading
- Independent Writing

explicit & modeled — structured & supported — automatic & natural unfamiliar word or when meaning breaks down. After the students read, the teacher gives a few teaching points (on-the-spot, targeted instruction) or has the students do some word work with words from the text. Guided reading lessons usually last approximately 25 to 30 minutes and occur three to five times per week.

WHAT GUIDED READING IS NOT

Most of us remember sitting in a reading group and taking turns reading aloud from a text in a format known as "round-robin reading," as we mentioned in our section on read-alouds. We can remember trying frantically to figure out which part we had to read in front of the group so we could practice it beforehand. We may also remember the humiliation when we had to read in front of everyone and we made mistakes or we could not read fluently. This format is different from guided reading, and it is not recommended (Miller, 2009; Freeman & Freeman, 2000; Optiz & Rasinski, 1998). A similar format to round-robin reading is "popcorn reading," which also has children reading aloud in front of their groups or even the whole class. The difference is that the student who is reading picks the next reader, so nobody knows what they will read in advance. Both of these practices can be detrimental to the reading process, causing students to experience anxiety and to dislike reading. In addition, little meaning is gleaned from the experience, as most students are not paying attention to others' reading, but they are rehearsing their own parts. Guided reading, on the other hand, focuses on setting students up for success by giving the right amount of support to make the reading successful and enjoyable.

THE BENEFITS OF GUIDED READING FOR ENGLISH LEARNERS

Because teachers give individualized instruction based upon each student's strengths and needs, guided reading is helpful for English learners just as it is for native English speakers. According to Fountas and Pinnell (2017), English learners "need teachers who understand their unique profile, and they need additional and different teaching" (p. 158). Older students, including older English learners who need more teacher support, also benefit from guided reading (Tompkins, 2014, p. 368). Peregoy and Boyle (2008) stress that English learners learn effectively through guided reading due to support from small groups, interesting texts at the correct level, and support from the teacher.

ACCOMMODATING GUIDED READING FOR ENGLISH LEARNERS

When introducing a new book to English learners, it is beneficial to use concrete objects and pictures to help students understand concepts and provide them extra practice with unfamiliar words or text structures (Fountas & Pinnell, 2017). It is also important to help English learners make connections to their prior knowledge through the book introduction, as it will help them bridge new information and vocabulary with what they already know (Suits, 2003; Fountas & Pinnell, 2017). Fountas and Pinnell (2017) suggest selecting texts that include vocabulary, concepts, and language structures that are within students' control, making sure not to include too much novel information. In addition, it is important to choose books that are culturally relevant for English language learners. For example, a child from India who is a vegetarian would not find much meaning or relevance in a book about a dog who visits the butcher and eats many different kinds of meat. Instead, it is preferable to find books that include children who resemble the children in the classroom and are about topics they find familiar and interesting. When this is not possible due to limited text selection, teachers can help English learners build the necessary background knowledge.

English learners also benefit from the lower teacher-to-student ratio that guided reading provides. Reducing the ratio allows the teacher to individualize instruction for students. Teachers are able to move at a pace that is practical for the students in the group. Students are also able to interact at a more intimate level with one another and with the teacher. This level of interaction increases student engagement as well as student participation.

A typical guided reading lesson might follow this format:

BEFORE READING:

Book Selection: The teacher chooses a book that is on the students' instructional reading level (can be read with 90 to 94% accuracy). All students in the group will be reading the same book, so multiple copies of the text are needed.

Book Introduction: The teacher leads students through a picture walk of the text, tells students what will happen in the book, and points out unfamiliar words. In addition, the teacher asks students to find familiar and unfamiliar words. The point of the book introduction is to provide enough information for students to read the book successfully with teacher support and sight word knowledge. In some cases, students may rehearse a part of the text that is either repeated or particularly difficult. For instance, in one story, *Blackberries*, a baby bear is picking blackberries, and he repeats, "Blackberries, blackberries! I love blackberries" (Randell, 2004). This might be something you would want students to practice. In another book, *The Hungry Giant*, a giant threatens to hit people with his "bommy-knocker"(Cowley, 2001). Most students would not be familiar with that word, so it is a good idea to discuss it beforehand. According to Clay (1993), "The child should know what the story is about before he reads it" (p. 37).

DURING READING:

The children read aloud simultaneously (not chorally, but independently), while the teacher listens closely to students one at a time.

The teacher responds to miscues or confusions with questions such as, "Does that make sense?" or "Does that look and sound right?" or "How can you help yourself?"

AFTER READING:

- The teacher encourages conversation about the book.
- The teacher gives compliments about a strategy used during the reading.
- The teacher presents teaching points about strategies that can be used when confusion occurs.
- The students participate in word work based on the text. An example of word work might be having students complete a word sort using word patterns or word families seen in the text or a word sort dealing with blends or digraphs from the text.
- The teacher reviews vocabulary from text.
- The students may also do some type of writing activity based on the text.
- The teacher encourages independent reading by placing books in book boxes or in the class library. One first grade teacher we know places small book baskets at each child's table containing the child's familiar books. Anytime during the day when children have a free moment, they are encouraged to read from their book baskets. Familiar books can also be read at the beginning of the next guided reading lesson for fluency practice.

	Before Reading	During Reading	After Reading
Teacher	Selects a text that matches students' level Introduces the book, giving information about plot, unfamiliar words, and patterns Reminds students of strategies they can use during the reading	Listens to students as they read, focusing on one at a time Observes students' reading behaviors Prompts students when unknown words or confusions occur	Compliments students on strategy use Encourages talk about the text Presents teaching points about strategies based on observations Reviews vocabulary from the text Gives word work based on the text Encourages rereading of the text
Students	Listen to book introduction Locate familiar and unfamiliar words in the text Rehearse sections of the text	Read entire text out loud Listen to teacher prompts Use reading strategies	Talk about the text Listen to teacher talk about strategy use Participate in word work guided by teacher Reread the text

First grade teacher Ms. Montrose has been doing guided reading groups with her students for several weeks. She has assigned students to groups based upon their reading levels and their reading needs. Throughout the year, groups will change as students develop differently as readers. As she is leading a guided reading group, Ms. Montrose ensures all other students are busily working with literacy centers or reading. On one particular day, Ms. Montrose calls her first guided reading group of the day: Julio (intermediate English proficiency level), Martha, Benjamin, Marcus (all native English speakers), and Maria (intermediate English proficiency level), who are all reading on the same reading level.

Ms. Montrose: *Have any of you ever wished that you could fly?*

Julio: *I dream I could fly.*

Benjamin: *I tried to fly once.*

Maria: *I fly in airplane.*

Marcus: *I pretended I flew when I was in my swing.*

Benjamin: *I wish I could fly.*

Martha: *Me too!*

Ms. Montrose: *Well, I have a book for you today about a man who could fly.*

She shows the students the cover of the book, *Dan, the Flying Man* (Cowley, 1990).

Ms. Montrose: *This is Dan, the Flying Man, and he can fly!*

Marcus: *He has a helicopter thingy on his head.*

Ms. Montrose: *Yes, he has a helicopter hat. Do you think that is what makes him fly?*

Children: *Yes!*

Ms. Montrose: *Well, Dan, the Flying Man flies all over the place! Let's look at the pictures and see where he flies.*

She shows the first page.

Ms. Montrose: *On this page, Dan says, "I am Dan, the Flying Man! Catch me! Catch me if you can!" Let's all read that together.*

Ms. Montrose and Children: *I am Dan, the Flying Man! Catch me! Catch me if you can!*

Ms. Montrose: *Look, on this page, he flies over houses. Maria, can you find the word "houses?"*

Maria points to the word "houses."

Ms. Montrose: *Read it, please.*

Maria: *Houses*

Ms. Montrose: *Nice reading, Maria. On this page, he flies over trees. Benjamin, can you show me the word "trees," please?*

Benjamin points to the word "trees."

Benjamin: *Trees.*

Ms. Montrose: *Nice job, Benjamin. On this page, he flies over mountains. Martha, can you show me the word "mountains," please?*

Martha points to the word "mountains."

Martha: *Mountains.*

Ms. Montrose: *Nice reading, Martha. Now, on this page, Dan says again, "I am Dan, the Flying Man! Catch me! Catch me if you can!" Let's read that all together.*

Ms. Montrose and Children: *I am Dan, the Flying Man! Catch me! Catch me if you can!*

Ms. Montrose: *Nice! Let's look on this page. Oh my! It tells us that all the people ran and ran, and they caught Dan, the Flying Man. Julio, where is that word, "caught?"*

Julio points to the word "caught."

Julio: *Caught.*

Ms. Montrose: *Nice! How did you know that word was "caught?"*

Julio: *C.*

Ms. Montrose: *Good noticing, Julio! Now, let's all read* Dan, the Flying Man. *When you get to a word you don't know, what can you try?*

Maria: *Read again.*

Ms. Montrose: *Yes! What else?*

Marcus: *Check the picture!*

Ms. Montrose: *Yes, good. What else can you do?*

Martha: *Start the word and read across it.*

Ms. Montrose: *Good! Now let's all read.*

Students read out loud quietly, and Ms. Montrose listens in to each student, one at a time. Julio reads, "Over a bridge and over a tried."

Ms. Montrose (to Julio): *Go back and reread, and think about what makes sense.*

Julio reads again and makes a self-correction reading the word "train."

Ms. Montrose: *Very nice correcting, Julio!*

Benjamin: *Tr-tr-t-r-tr*

Ms. Montrose (to Benjamin): *Check the picture.*

Benjamin: *Train!*

Ms. Montrose: *Good job! I like the way you checked the picture.*

Maria: *Miss, I'm finish!*

Ms. Montrose: *Oh, that's great, Maria! Now go back and read it again.*

All students finish reading.

Ms. Montrose: *Everyone did such a nice job. I saw Julio go back and reread when he wasn't sure of a word. When he read it the second time, he read the word "train!" Good job, Julio. I also saw Benjamin check the picture when he came to a word he didn't know, and I saw Martha run her finger under a word, look closely at it, and sound it out. Then she said the first letter and read the word. Those are all things good readers do! Now what do you think about the story?*

Martha: *I liked how he flew all over. When you swing high, you can see lots of things also!*

Ms. Montrose: *Yes, you're right! Good connection!*

Benjamin: *Dan, the Flying Man, flew everywhere and looked at mountains and houses!*

Ms. Montrose: *That's right! He did look at lots of things.*

Maria: *And people caught him!*

Ms. Montrose: *That's right! Now I have a word sort for all of you to do.*

She gives the children word cards with "tr" words and words without "tr." Students work in pairs to sort the words with "tr" and those without. After the lesson, Ms. Montrose puts the books in the book center for the students to read. The next day, she will have the students in this group read the book again as a familiar book.

WHAT THE EXPERTS SAY

Fountas and Pinnell (1996) state that through guided reading, "teachers can show children how to read and can support children as they read" (p. 1). With the teacher's support, students are able to learn strategies that enable them to read independently and develop automaticity, according to the authors. The teacher is able to observe students as they read in order to determine strategy and cueing system use (semantic, syntactic, and graphophonic) and thereby establish students' need for strategy instruction and word work.

Teachers tailor their specific responses to meet individual students' needs while focusing on their strengths (Fountas & Pinnell, 2017). In guided reading, teachers set students up for success by choosing a book on their reading level, providing a strong book introduction, and giving support in the form of prompts during the reading. Additionally, guided reading provides students social interaction with other readers while they participate in the reading process (Fountas & Pinnell, 1996).

According to Tompkins (2014), guided reading provides a level of scaffolding in which students are actually reading and receiving assistance and instruction at the same time. It is important for students to read books at their instructional level (90 to 94% accuracy), so they can read through the book with the support of the book introduction, teacher prompting, and their own

knowledge of sight words and strategies (Fountas & Pinnell, 2017). Reading levels can be assessed through running records and miscue analysis. Tompkins emphasizes that books at too low of a reading level are not challenging enough for students and do not require them to use their strategies, while books at too high of a reading level are frustrating for students. With careful attention to book selection, teachers can help students progress through books of increasing difficulty and grow in independence (Clay, 1993).

Fountas and Pinnell (1996) describe how some children seem to learn to read with very little effort. Others develop their knowledge of reading in different ways and need

extra help as they learn to use strategies to access different sources. According to Clay (1993), these sources of information fall into three cueing systems: meaning cues, structural cues, and visual cues. Meaning or semantic cues deal with readers' knowledge of the world and how they make sense of the text. Structural or syntactic cues deal with the way words are put together into sentences following the rules of English. Visual cues or graphophonic cues are related to the alphabetic principle—that letters represent sounds and that they go together from left to right to make words.

By teaching strategies through mini-lessons and prompting during the reading, teachers can give students access to the cueing systems. For example, to help students access meaning cues, the teacher might say, "Think about what makes sense." To help students establish structural cues, the teacher could say, "Can we say it that way?" To help students pay attention to visual cues, the teacher could say, "Do you know a word that starts with that letter?" or "Start the word and read across it."

Students "crosscheck" between cueing systems to verify their strategy use (Clay, 1993). Fountas and Pinnell (1996) emphasize that correct reading is not as important as developing a self-extending system that enables students to use different sources of information and monitor their own reading. Fountas and Pinnell (2017) also warn against interrupting the reading too much, trying to correct every miscue, or teaching too much new information at once, as it is likely to slow students' momentum. The more students practice using these strategies with support from the teacher, the more independent they become, and the more they start to access the cueing systems on their own. Guided reading is an excellent way for students to develop automaticity with the guidance of their teachers and become independent, fluent, strategic readers (Fountas & Pinnell, 1996).

Cueing System	Prompts
Meaning (semantic)	Does it make sense? What happened in the story when...? What do you think it might be?
Structure (syntactic)	Does it sound right? Can we say it that way? What is another word that might fit there?
Visual (graphophonic)	Does it look right? Do you recognize any word parts? Do you know another word that might start that way?

Guided Reading Lesson Map

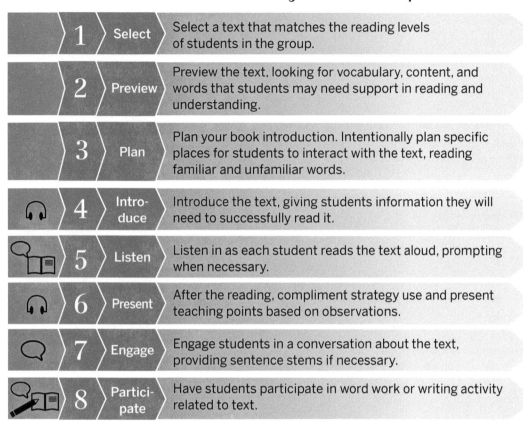

	1	Select	Select a text that matches the reading levels of students in the group.
	2	Preview	Preview the text, looking for vocabulary, content, and words that students may need support in reading and understanding.
	3	Plan	Plan your book introduction. Intentionally plan specific places for students to interact with the text, reading familiar and unfamiliar words.
🎧	4	Introduce	Introduce the text, giving students information they will need to successfully read it.
💬📖	5	Listen	Listen in as each student reads the text aloud, prompting when necessary.
🎧	6	Present	After the reading, compliment strategy use and present teaching points based on observations.
💬	7	Engage	Engage students in a conversation about the text, providing sentence stems if necessary.
✏️📖	8	Participate	Have students participate in word work or writing activity related to text.

FAQ

How do I determine which students should be in each guided reading group?

A guided reading group should be made up of four to five students with similar reading behaviors who read on the same or similar reading levels. Grouping should be flexible and dynamic, rather than fixed. Fountas and Pinnell also teach us that students are "grouped and regrouped in a dynamic process that involves ongoing observation and assessment" (1996, p. 4). For English learners and students who struggle, it is especially important to ensure that groups are constantly changing to alleviate any sort of stigma associated with membership in any particular group. In addition, Smith and Elley (1994) emphasize the importance of children being members of a community of readers who support each other as they develop as independent readers. A guided reading group provides this sense of community for children as they share the reading experience. Additionally, Tompkins (2014) stresses the value of English learners working with native English speakers in small groups. The author states, "English learners talk with classmates as they read and write, and at the same time, they are learning the culture of literacy" (p. 30).

Are my students too old for guided reading?

Older students can benefit from guided reading as well. Guided reading provides extra small-group support when students are reading below grade level for the purpose of accelerating reading growth. This is especially beneficial if students are new to the country and learning English.

How do I choose a book for a guided reading group?

The best answer to this is to know your students! It is important to be aware of students' reading behaviors, known sight words, and interests in order to make the best book selection for them. At the beginning of the school year, teachers can determine initial reading levels with the Fountas and Pinnell Assessment System (2017), a published reading inventory, or their district's reading assessment. Once teachers know the instructional reading levels of their students, they can group the students based upon level, reading behaviors, and interest. Once students are assigned to groups, the teacher can choose a book that members of the group can read successfully with the teacher's support. It is essential to know the texts and what students will need to know in order to read the text with success (Fountas & Pinnell, 2017). Fountas and Pinnell also suggest that teachers "puzzle out what a reader has to do to read the text with comprehension, accuracy, and fluency" (p. 20). Teachers can monitor text levels of all students with running records and close observation in order to move students from group to group as their reading behaviors, sight word knowledge, and interests change throughout the school year.

How detailed should the book introduction be?

Again, knowing your students is key. Learners in the earlier stages of reading and English learners need a more detailed book introduction than those who have developed more reading behaviors and who read more independently in English at higher levels

One year, we had a new student join our third grade class in January. He was from Brazil and was completely literate in Portuguese. This student could read, write, listen, and speak fluently in his primary language. Learning to do the same in English was his newest journey, and we were honored to be part of it. Because of the firm foundation he had in his first language, he could transfer many of those skills to his new language. For example, he already knew that letters make sounds, that we read left to right, that words and sentences make meaning, and much more. Guided reading allowed me to take him from where he was to the next level.

—Valentina

of difficulty. In addition, book introductions vary based upon text characteristics and interests, strengths, and needs of the readers in the group. The level of support needed from the teacher decreases as a child's reading proficiency increases. Readers need enough information from the book introduction to help them read the book successfully with their word knowledge, strategy use, knowledge of cueing systems, and support from the teacher. Less experienced readers will need a much more detailed book introduction than those who have developed more independence. In particular, it is important to give English language learners support with vocabulary and language structure. Fountas and Pinnell (1996) state that the book introduction "debugs the book for the children by directing their attention to new text features they will need to use as readers" (p. 8).

Book introductions are much like movie trailers. Seeing a movie trailer gives us an overall view of the movie. It provides anticipation and a desire to watch the movie. Then while watching the movie, we tend to look for parts that connect with the trailer. A book introduction, like a movie trailer, gives readers background knowledge and taps into prior knowledge, linking what students know to what they will learn.

What should the instruction after the story look like?

This depends on how the reading went and what you observed as your students were reading. You will most likely see something you want to include as a teaching point or bring to the students' attention. For example, if a child makes a self-correction, you may want to draw the groups' attention to that as an example of what good readers do. In addition, you can encourage conversation about the text. With the text fresh in their minds, students are able to use language structures from the text to discuss ideas about what they have just read. This is especially important for English learners, as they are able to participate in an authentic conversation with their peers by using text language. You can provide sentence stems to promote conversation by giving students access to academic language. Some examples may include: "In my opinion…," "I agree/disagree because…," and "One thing I noticed is…" (Seidlitz & Perryman, 2011; Fountas & Pinnell, 2017).

In addition, students benefit from doing word work to learn about how words

One first grader I taught read the word "look" in a book he was reading for guided reading. He told me that the word "look" rhymes with the word "book." Because of this, I decided to have the group do 'Making and Breaking Words' with the word "look" and see how many words they could think of. They came up with the words, "book," "cook," "hook," and "kook." The kids talked about how most of the words rhymed except for the word "kook." They remarked how it was interesting that the words had the same spelling pattern but sounded different. I then went back to the word "look" and had them find it in the book to relate the activity back to the literature.

— Melinda

work and how you can read a new word by applying something you know from another word. For example, students can do word sorts, making and breaking words, or analogies. Though writing is not always a part of a guided reading lesson, it is beneficial for students to participate in some type of writing activity such as interactive writing or shared writing. This writing would give students another avenue for using the vocabulary and language structure of the text and processing their thinking about the text (Fountas & Pinnell, 2017).

How do I know my students are successful in guided reading?
By observing students' reading behaviors and performing running records on students, you will be able to monitor students' use of strategies and track their progress through reading levels. If learners are reading texts of increasing difficulty and displaying use of strategies, their experience with guided reading can be deemed successful. The ulti-

mate test is whether or not the guided reading lesson is based upon students' needs and helps them develop as independent readers.

How often should I meet with each guided reading group?
The answer is as often as possible! Fountas and Pinnell (1996) recommend that younger children in the earlier stages of reading participate in guided reading three to five times per week in order to maintain progress through reading levels. English learners and all learners who need extra support should have the opportunity to take part in guided reading as often as possible. In guided reading, every student listens to the book introduction and teacher prompting, reads the entire book, talks about the book and strategy use, and often participates in some type of word work or writing activity about the book. The more English learners use their new language, the more quickly they will learn to listen, speak, read, and write in English (Seidlitz & Perryman, 2011; Tompkins, 2014).

Supporting English Learners at Various English Proficiency Levels in Guided Reading

WIDA
ELPA 21
ELPS/TELPAS

ENTERING	EMERGING	DEVELOPING/ EXPANDING	BRIDGING/ REACHING
1	2	3	4/5
Beginning	Intermediate	Advanced	Advanced High
• Provide simple sentence stems for opportunities to talk • Give clear, one step directions • Preview side-by-side text in primary language • Build vocabulary using visuals, illustration, gestures, realia • Use shared reading • Allow ample wait time	• Provide simple sentence stems for opportunities to talk • Ask "yes" and "no" questions • Build vocabulary using visuals, illustration, gestures, realia • Use shared reading • Select predictable texts	• Provide complex sentence stems for opportunities to talk • Ask "why" and "how" questions • Build vocabulary using visuals and gestures as needed • Allow ample wait time • Select highly engaging, compelling texts	• Provide complex sentence stems for opportunities to talk • Ask "why do you think..." and "what would happen if..." questions • Build vocabulary using visuals and gestures as needed • Allow ample wait time • Select highly engaging, compelling texts

English learners should have the opportunity to take part in guided reading as often as possible.

Chapter 6

Independent Reading

"**Any book** that helps a child to form a habit of reading, to make reading one of his deep and continuing needs, is **good** for him."

– Maya Angelou

WHAT IS INDEPENDENT READING?

In our classrooms, independent reading looks like students reading individually from books they've self-selected. In many classrooms, independent reading happens daily for 10 to 30 minutes. Students hold their own copies of the text and read either silently or in a whisper.

Independent reading is part of the "YOU DO" stage in the Gradual Release of Responsibility. At this point, we have already modeled for students what proficient reading sounds like and how to think and navigate through print. Now that we have practiced with them, it's their turn to read on their own.

When I think about my own experiences with independent reading, it takes me back to third grade in the '80s. I had a great reading teacher. Looking back now, I can see that he was progressive for his time. Every day, he asked us to read out of our own self-selected books. We all got to pick a spot anywhere we wanted in the room. Some curled up under their desks, some picked cozy corners, and others nestled in the fun seats he had for us. Me, I stayed in my own chair at my own desk. I grabbed the book that I'd been required to check out from the library, and each day I opened to a random page. I peered over the book and glanced at the other kids. What were they doing? Why were they so enthralled? I didn't get it. The problem for me was that I struggled with reading on my own, so independent reading time was a waste of time most days. If only my teacher knew. If only he could see what was going on in my head. What could have been the solution? You've probably realized it by now. The solution could have been to confer with me and work with me one-on-one or in a small group. I probably needed some direct teaching of reading strategies to help strengthen me as a reader. Clearly, I wanted to do well. I sat attentively, I observed what others were doing and copied them but I couldn't understand what was invisible to me. "What's going on in their heads?" I wondered. That's what I needed from my teacher.

—*Valentina*

A FRAMEWORK FOR K-5 77

Assigning a chapter in a book or assigning students books by their reading level is not independent reading. Though it may seem like these two acts are effective, they do little to help students grow as readers. Fountas and Pinnell (2017) remind us that when students are reading independently, they "have full control of the process in independent reading, although you support them by offering a rich, well-organized collection of books from which to choose" (p. 39). Knowing students' reading levels is helpful for us as teachers. We can use that information for guided reading groups, but students don't need to know their levels.

Independent reading must involve more than simply unsupervised reading without feedback. The teacher and students play active roles in independent reading. If we value independent reading, then we will be right alongside them, guiding them, conferring with them, gathering in small groups, taking notes, etc. Independent reading is the time for us to gather information to drive our small-group instruction, which is the heart of the work we do with students. When teachers are not part of the independent reading process, administrators may question the value of independent reading. It also sends the wrong message to students. Students watch us. They know what we value by how we act.

Sometimes schools may already have designated times for silent reading, such as DEAR (Drop Everything And Read) and SSR (Sustained Silent Reading). Typically during DEAR and SSR, the teacher's role does not involve conferring or gathering students for small-group instruction. While these programs may be very valuable on their own, independent reading time within a workshop model involves the teacher taking an active role during time set aside for independent reading.

Gradual Release of Responsibility & Components of Literacy

I do	We do	You do
• Mini-Lesson	• Shared Reading	★ Independent Reading
• Read-Aloud	• Guided Reading	• Independent Writing
• Write-Aloud	• Shared Writing	

explicit & modeled	structured & supported	automatic & natural

THE BENEFITS OF INDEPENDENT READING FOR ENGLISH LEARNERS

Independent reading offers teachers a time to work with individual students and meet them wherever they are on the reading continuum. Teachers are able to confer one-on-one or gather students with similar needs and provide explicit instruction.

English learners especially benefit from the rich vocabulary in books they read. The majority of vocabulary growth happens not as a result of direct instruction but as a result of reading voluminously (Cunningham & Zibulsky, 2014).

"Independent reading is an essential practice, one that develops background knowledge, improves fluency and comprehension, heightens motivation, increases reading achievement, and helps students broaden their vocabulary" (Miller & Moss, 2013, p. 11-12). In addition, it has a significant effect on language acquisition (Krashen, 1993).

Goldenberg and Coleman (2010) state that "reading comprehension requires not only reading skills—accurate and fluent word recognition, understanding how words form but also fundamental language proficiency—knowledge of vocabulary, syntax, and conventions of use that are the essence of 'knowing' a language. Learners who know the language can concentrate on the academic content. But learners who do not know the language, or do not know it well enough, must devote part of their attention to learning and understand the very language in which that content is taught" (p. 50).

ACCOMMODATING INDEPENDENT READING FOR ENGLISH LEARNERS

Routman (2003) says, "Just adding more time and space for independent reading is not enough" (p. 83). We can't assume that students will improve just by giving them more time to read. More time doesn't ensure that students will understand the books that are in their hands, nor does it ensure that they are actually reading behind the pages. Monitoring student progress and providing feedback during independent reading is critical for English learners.

Research from the National Literacy Panel found that English learners' literacy achievement was enhanced by providing familiar reading materials (Goldenberg & Coleman, 2010).

To set students up for success, we can accommodate independent reading in many ways:

- Working frequently with students in small groups for direct instruction
- Setting a purpose for reading
- Building stamina by slowly increasing the amount of time reading
- Providing opportunities for students to talk about the books they are reading
- Conferring frequently with students to check for gaps, book matching, phonics needs, etc.
- Tapping into the strengths and culture of the students in our classrooms
- Providing books that are inclusive of all students
- Allowing choice in reading, including native language texts
- Providing familiar reading materials

Supporting **ENGLISH** Learners *Independent* in **Reading**

@ValentinaESL

Provide books that tap into students' cultures & passions

Set a purpose

work frequently in small groups with students for explicit & direct instruction

Allow choice

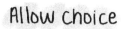

Provide familiar reading materials

Build stamina

Create space for peer-to-peer book discussions

CLASSROOM SCENARIO

Walking into Ms. Dunlavy's class, we see students scattered around the room, nestled with books and pillows in every corner. Some students sit with classmates and others sit alone, yet they are all intently reading books from different genres that they have chosen. Ms. Dunlavy is traveling around the room carrying a notebook. She goes from one student to another and stops at one particular child, Fatima, an ESL student who has been in the program since kindergarten and is at a high level of proficiency.

Ms. Dunlavy: *Hi Fatima, can you tell me about the book you're reading?*

Fatima: *I am reading* Hank the Cowdog. *I really like it because it is about a dog.*

She continues, describing the chapter she just read.

Ms. Dunlavy: *Fatima, can you please choose a page from your book to read to me?*

Ms. Dunlavy observes and takes anecdotal notes about Fatima's reading. She plans to use those when gathering small groups later this week. Then she walks over to Esteban, a student who is at a beginning proficiency level in English, and smiles.

Ms. Dunlavy: *Hi, Esteban. Can I sit with you?*

Ms. Dunlavy is careful with her body language and uses gestures to support Esteban's comprehension. She wants Esteban to feel comfortable. This is about building relationships while also learning about Esteban's literacy.

Esteban nods, and Mrs. Dunlavy sits and points to the book.

Ms. Dunlavy: *What are you reading?*

Esteban: *Volcán.*

He points to a picture of a volcano on the cover of the book.

Ms. Dunlavy: *Can you read to me?*

Ms. Dunlavy makes a talking gesture with her hands and points to a page from the book. Esteban reads, and Ms. Dunlavy listens and takes notes.

Ms. Dunlavy: *You read that very nicely, Esteban! Can you tell me how volcanoes are made?*

Esteban responds in Spanish and draws a picture. Though Ms. Dunlavy cannot speak Spanish, she is able to see that Esteban is comprehending and that he's excited about reading on this topic.

Finally, Ms. Dunlavy gathers a small group of students. During independent reading, teachers have the ability to confer one-on-one with students, gather guided reading groups, or work with small groups on a common skill. Using data she gathered from anecdotal notes from last week as she conferred one-on-one with students, she found that this group of students all had a similar need in reading. Their reading goal is to effectively communicate a retelling. Ms. Dunlavy conducted a quick mini-lesson on retelling. Then she gave them an opportunity to practice as a group with her guidance. Ms. Dunlavy supported her group with sentence stems as they used their own books to practice retelling with a partner.

WHAT THE EXPERTS SAY

Fountas and Pinnell (2017) state that independent reading allows students to "develop tastes as a reader and to read a large number of self-selected books with the support of individual conferences with the teacher."

"Giving kids time to read is necessary, not optional. And giving them the chance to discover what they want to read is also necessary. When schools choose not to do those things, they are simply failing to provide a good literacy education (Beers & Probst, 2017, p. 136). Gallagher (2009) emphasizes, "When schools deprive students of the pleasures of recreational reading, we end up graduating test-takers who may never again read for pleasure" (p. 45).

Marinak and Gambrell remind us that confining students to reading levels limits their reading lives. They posit that children do not possess a single reading level. They are able to read material of varying levels, depending upon prior knowledge, interests, support, and tenacity (2016). According to Gallagher, "...students are in desperate need of large doses of authentic reading" (p. 29). Students should be given daily opportunities to read a variety of interesting, culturally relevant reading materials including fiction, nonfiction, newspapers, magazines, comic books, novels, graphic novels, blogs, and websites. Gallagher states, "Our students should be reading through many windows, not just a single, narrow window that gives them a view of the next exam" (p. 29).

Students' reading ability has a positive impact on their writing. Wright (2015) shows that "reading becomes more and more important to students' writing development as they gain proficiency in English" (p. 226). Reading and writing support one another. As students read, they gain vocabulary and language structures they transfer to their writing.

Independent Reading Lesson Map

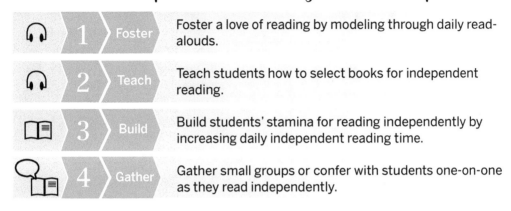

1 Foster Foster a love of reading by modeling through daily read-alouds.

2 Teach Teach students how to select books for independent reading.

3 Build Build students' stamina for reading independently by increasing daily independent reading time.

4 Gather Gather small groups or confer with students one-on-one as they read independently.

Should students read independently every day?

The goal in an effective, balanced literacy program is for students to read independently every day. This can be challenging when students have not yet acquired the stamina and fluency necessary to be engaged independently with a book for long periods of time. It is important to allow students to read independently for periods of time in which they can do so successfully, especially in the early phases of setting up this dedicated time.

What will I do while students are reading independently?

The teacher's role during independent reading is vital. You can choose to do one of two things as students read independently: confer or gather a small group. Some teachers like to set aside specific days for conferring with students and other days for gathering small groups for guided reading. For example, Monday and Wednesday could be conferring days, and Tuesday, Thursday, and Friday could be small group days.

As you confer, keep anecdotal notes. These notes will help you plan instruction and grouping for small groups. For example, if you observed four students who struggled with inferring characters' feelings, you might gather these students for a small group to directly teach this skill.

How will I know if students are really reading and not just faking it?

You will get good at noticing this very quickly as you meet with students to confer with them. Conferring involves a three to five minute talk, and it simply serves as an opportunity to see how things are going and to build relationships with your learners. You might ask students to read a page of their books. You could compliment them on something they did well and then coach them on something they could improve upon.

What kinds of books should students read?

Students benefit from a classroom library that includes books from all genres and books of different lengths, too. Making all types of literature accessible to students will help them find the right match. This includes fiction, nonfiction, poetry, folktales, comics, graphic novels, series, fantasy, chapter books, picture books, new books, familiar reads, and more.

We know some teachers might be thinking, *"Students have to read texts that are required. So it's better that they get used to it."* We understand that. But if we equip them with a love of reading first, then when it's time to read what is required, they will be prepared.

Offering students a wide variety of high-quality books will help them make choices that fit them best. If we want students to read, they have to find books that they will stick with and enjoy. Look through your bookshelf and see if your books reflect the students in your classroom. Students who connect with books they read tend to bond with them better.

Build a classroom library that represents the students in your classroom. It is important for all students to be able to see themselves in the literature. Some teachers like to survey their class at the beginning of the year to find out about students' interests and cultures and match books to them. (See Appendix 128 for a list of culturally inclusive books that we recommend.)

How do students select books for independent reading?

Some teachers start the year with a lesson on selecting books that are just right—books that are a match for their students based not only on their readability but also on their ability to connect to students' interests. For example, if a student loves cars, he may choose a book on cars that is above his reading level. That's okay because his desire to learn about cars is so great that he may push himself. We don't want to limit kids by only allowing them to select books based on our assessment of their current reading levels.

What if by teaching in small groups I miss teaching important skills that my students need?

There's a concern that if teachers only teach lessons to students in small groups or one-on-one, certain skills and concepts will be lost or won't be taught and gaps will form. This is a valid concern, and we certainly don't want this to happen. It's important to build on skills in reading. For this reason, reading can be taught using a combination of whole-group and small-group teaching. Lessons can be introduced to the whole group initially and then taught more intensely in small groups as needed for those who require a follow up or reteach.

Supporting English Learners at Various English Proficiency Levels in Independent Reading

WIDA
ELPA 21
ELPS/TELPAS

ENTERING	EMERGING	DEVELOPING/ EXPANDING	BRIDGING/ REACHING
1	2	3	4/5
Beginning	Intermediate	Advanced	Advanced High
• Confer with student frequently • Practice echo and shared reading methods in small groups • Provide support with phonics and concepts of print in English • Provide books in student's primary language • Offer familiar texts and poems for IR • Place student in a triad with a same-language-speaking peer and an English speaking peer for book discussions	• Confer with student frequently • Practice echo and shared reading methods in small groups • Allow books in student's primary language • Provide opportunities for student to discuss reading with a partner	• Confer with student regularly • Provide self-selected book choice with teacher guidance • Cocreate reading goals with the student	• Confer with student regularly • Provide self-selected book choice with teacher guidance • Cocreate reading goals with the student

Chapter 7

Write-Aloud

> "When I began to *write*, I found this was the best way to make sense out of my life."
>
> *- John Cheever*

WHAT IS A WRITE-ALOUD?

A write-aloud is a writing demonstration in which the teacher verbalizes her thoughts as a writer while modeling the writing process. Write-aloud can be done with a document camera, on chart paper, or even on the whiteboard, and it represents the highest level of support given through scaffolding.

Since the teacher is doing a majority of the talking, it is important for students to have frequent opportunities to turn and talk to their neighbors about what the teacher is saying and doing. One way to boost the power of write-aloud is to have students chorally read portions of the text the teacher has written. It is helpful if the teacher uses high-frequency words that students can easily read with support.

Gradual Release of Responsibility & Components of Literacy

I do → **We do** → **You do**

• Mini-Lesson	• Shared Reading	• Independent Reading
• Read-Aloud	• Guided Reading	• Independent Writing
⭐ Write-Aloud	• Shared Writing	

explicit & modeled → **structured & supported** → **automatic & natural**

WHAT A WRITE-ALOUD IS NOT

A write-aloud is not a lecture, and it is not necessarily a lengthy activity. Most importantly, a write-aloud is not only teacher talk. Students should be able to talk to their peers and teacher about what they are seeing and hearing and to read the text chorally after the teacher writes.

Another misconception about write-alouds is that premade writing can be used in lieu of writing in front of the students. **Though sharing examples is effective, premade writing does not support the write-aloud process. The power in write-alouds lies in the way we make them while students observe.** They are able to witness how an idea grows into a piece of writing.

THE BENEFITS OF WRITE-ALOUDS FOR ENGLISH LEARNERS

Write-alouds benefit English learners because they are able to hear and see demonstrations of what happens during the composition process. It is beneficial for the teacher to use high-frequency words during the teacher's think-aloud while writing to enable English learners to make connections to what they already know. In addition, chorally reading and talking to peers about what the teacher is saying and writing will provide support for English learners.

WRITE-ALOUDS ACHIEVE THE FOLLOWING:

- Make thinking visible
- Demonstrate examples of English language structures
- Provide explicit instruction
- Support language development
- Build vocabulary
- Offer authentic grammar practice

ACCOMMODATING WRITE-ALOUDS FOR ENGLISH LEARNERS

Since the write-aloud is highly teacher centered, it is important to keep tabs on how well English learners comprehend the teacher talk. To ensure that what we say during the teacher talk is accessible to students, we can slow down the rate of speech and enunciate carefully. In addition, using gestures and visual supports may help to make input more comprehensible to English learners.

Balancing the amount of teacher talk with peer-to-peer discussion can also promote language development and academic success. Providing students with frequent, structured opportunities to turn and talk with a partner during the write-aloud will promote comprehension. They can engage in discussion with their partners about the content of the writing or about a feature of the text. For example, the teacher may ask students to discuss word choice or punctuation. On the other hand, the teacher could ask students to summarize, retell, or give an opinion of what has been written.

Some students may benefit from hearing and saying the words aloud. Echo and/or choral reading are excellent ways to actively engage students in reading the text as a class, building fluency, and practicing English language structures.

A typical write-aloud might follow this format:

Mr. Menil calls his third grade students to come and sit on the carpet for a write-aloud. He has taken them through several write-alouds, and he is encouraging his students to write about what they know and what they love. He frequently shares stories with the class about his pets and gives them opportunities to tell stories about their animals, their families, and the things they do at home.

Mr. Menil: *My cat, Scarlett, did the funniest thing this morning, and I just have to write about it. In fact, I think that is how I want to start my writing piece: "Scarlett did something funny this morning." Now I know I should start the sentence with a capital letter, and "Scarlett" would be capital anyway because it is a name, right?"*

Students: *Right!*

Mr. Menil writes "Scarlett did something funny this morning."

Mr. Menil: *Now, I want to jump right in and say what the funny thing was, so the reader will be interested. I am going to write, "She hid behind the couch and jumped out at me when I walked by."*

Mr. Menil writes **"She hid behind the couch and jumped out at me when I walked by."**

Samuel: *What happened next?*

Mr. Menil: *Well, she jumped at me, but she didn't notice my dog, Copper, walking between my feet. She landed on him instead, then sprang into the air hissing!*

Bridgett: *Write that!*

Mr. Menil: *Ok, I want to make it sound really funny, so I think I will write, "I think she intended to ambush me, but instead, she landed on Copper, who was walking between my legs. She was so surprised, she sprang into the air with a loud hiss." I want to make it sound as funny as possible, so I will write about what Scarlett might have been thinking.*

Toby: *That's good! That's funny.*

Mr. Menil writes "I think she intended to ambush me, but instead, she landed on Copper, who was walking between my legs. She was so surprised, she sprang into the air with a loud hiss." Students laugh.

Mr. Menil: *So why do you think I used the words, "She sprang into the air with a loud hiss?" Turn to your neighbors, and tell them why I did that. I'm listening for sentences like, "I think Mr. Menil used those words because..."*

Students talk to their shoulder partners. Mr. Menil randomizes and draws Yolanda's popsicle stick.

Mr. Menil: *Yolanda, what did you and your partner say?*

Yolanda: *You did that so we could picture what it looked like when she jumped.*

Mr. Menil: *Right, so why did I use the word, "ambushed?"*

Bridgett: *I think it sounds funnier than just jumping.*

Mr. Menil: *You think so? I do, too. Now let's go back and look and see if I have capitals and punctuation where they belong. Let's read it all together.*

All read.

Samuel: *Maybe you could put an exclamation point after "hiss." That would make it really funny.*

Mr. Menil: *Oh, that's a good idea, Samuel. That will make it funnier.*

Mr. Menil adds an exclamation point.

Mr. Menil: *Ok, does everything look right?*

Students: *Yes!*

Mr. Menil: *Ok, now let's go back and read it again, and when we get to the exclamation point, we will read it with an excited voice!*

All read.

Mr. Menil: *Oh, that sounded so good with the exclamation point. Now, I bet all of you can think of something funny that happened to you that you would like to write about! Before we go off to write, let's talk to our partners about the stories we might write about.*

Students share with their partners before heading off to write.

WHAT THE EXPERTS SAY

Cooper and Kiger (2003) describe the modes of writing, which include write-aloud, shared writing, and independent writing. The authors' ideas are based on Pearson's (1985) idea of Gradual Release of Responsibility from teacher to student. If teachers model metacognition as well as skills and procedures, students will ultimately emulate them and become successful writers.

Gallagher (2011) emphasizes that he provides students with examples of writing before he asks them to write. Graves (1983) states, "The objective of composing before children is to make explicit what children ordinarily can't see: how words go down on paper, and the thoughts that go with the decisions made in writing" (p. 45). Routman (1994) states that writing aloud is helpful as a demonstration technique at any grade level and recommends modeling the thought processes involving different aspects of writing, including format, spelling, punctuation, vocabulary, spacing, and handwriting.

One example of a write-aloud Routman describes is the "Morning Message." While writing a meaningful message to students on the upcoming happenings of the day, the teacher asks such questions as, "Why did I capitalize…? Why did I begin the paragraph here? Why did I use a comma?, and What did you notice about…?" (p. 51). Students answer these questions rather than the teacher doing all of the talking. Routman quotes one second grade teacher as saying, "I feel writing aloud with my students clearly puts so many of the conventions we want to teach children in the proper context of written language without teaching the skills in isolation" (p. 52).

Fletcher and Portalupi (2001) stress the importance of students watching an adult write while they are learning to write. Somehow, it becomes less intimidating, and students seem more motivated when they see their teachers write, too. Routman (2005) stresses that the more modeling the teacher does, the more excited students will be about writing, and the better their writing will become. When a teacher demonstrates high-quality writing, students know what is expected of them, and they are more engaged and more willing to write. In addition, they come up with more and more of their own ideas of what to write about. Routman offers these tips for teachers when they are writing aloud:

> **"Be yourself.**
> Write about what interests you.
>
> **Write the same exciting story you tell orally**. Include the details that make the story come alive.
>
> Don't get distracted by kids' questions. Keep writing.
>
> **Don't go on so long you exhaust the students.** Stop while they're still engaged."
>
> (p. 181).

Cooper (2000) recommends that teachers begin teaching the writing process through write-aloud, then gradually release more and more responsibility to the students as they begin to become more independent writers. He notes that write-aloud can be used at any grade level to help students learn new types of writing and learn to problem-solve as they are writing.

Graves (1983) explains that his relationship with his students takes on a new tone when he demonstrates the composing process to them. He becomes part of their community of writers, and they support and encourage each other through the problem-solving involved in the writing process.

Write-Aloud Lesson Map

1	Choose	Choose a purpose for your write-aloud based on students' needs and state standards.
2	Select	Select an engaging topic for your write-aloud.
3	Gather	Gather students, and prepare to write on a whiteboard, document camera, or chart paper.
4	Introduce	Introduce write-aloud to students, telling them why you decided to write this.
5	Verbalize	Verbalize thoughts, and write simultaneously.
6	Provide	Provide opportunities for students to verbalize.
7	Engage	Engage students in chorally reading the writing.
8	Write	Ask students to write using the model you provided.

FAQ

How often should I do write-alouds?

The answer is as often as possible! The more you demonstrate writing and writing conventions through write-aloud for your students, the more engaged they will become, and the better writers they will become (Routman, 2005).

Won't writing aloud take up a lot of time?

Write-aloud can be as short or long as you want it to be. Routman (1994) describes a teacher who said she couldn't possibly do a write-aloud on a regular basis because of the strict daily schedule. When she tried it for herself, she was pleasantly surprised at how little time it actually took.

Should I make mistakes in my write-aloud on purpose and see if the kids notice?

This is up to the individual teacher. Routman (1994) believes that it is always important to write in our best form as an example of good writing for students, so she does not recommend making deliberate mistakes. Other teachers make a few mistakes on purpose to show students the editing process. We recommend being up-front with students and explaining that you will be making some mistakes in order to demonstrate to them what to do if they make a mistake.

What if I am not a very good writer myself?

Many teachers do not see themselves as writers and do not feel confident teaching writing or writing in front of their students. The truth is, the more you write, the better writer you will become. It takes practice, just like anything else. It might be a good idea to think of a funny story, like the one in the scenario, and practice what you plan to write before you write it as a write-aloud for your students. The main thing to remember is to have fun with it and let your voice shine through. Your students will love seeing you as a writer!

What if students just copy what I write?

They might, especially at first. But you can gradually guide them to hear their own voices as they write (Painter, 2006). This is all part of the process. As students become accustomed to having time to write and freedom to choose what to write about, they will begin to come up with their own ideas.

I always used my pets as my topic for write-aloud. My first and second graders were always excited to hear stories about my pets, and I knew they would be interested if I did that for a write-aloud. Many times, it helped them think of funny episodes involving their own pets, and those became their writing topics!

— Melinda

Painter suggests having students turn to their neighbors and share what their writing topics are, then having a few students share out loud. On the occasion that a student picks the topic you have just written about, you can say something like, "Oh, good! I can't wait to hear how yours is different from mine!" (Painter, 2006).

When should I use a write-aloud?

We suggest using a write-aloud every time you want to teach your students something new about writing. You can use write-aloud to demonstrate how to go through the writing process. In addition, you can do a daily morning message as a write-aloud for younger students. For older students, you can even use write-aloud to show what is expected of them when doing a specific genre or assignment (Routman, 1994). When students know what is expected of them, they are more comfortable with writing and more motivated.

How can I support English learners who struggle with English language structures?

Some languages do not share the same patterns that English has. For instance, they may put the adjective after the noun. In other cases, the classroom may be the only place where they are exposed to large amounts of spoken English.

One technique that scaffolds learning for ELs who are acquiring English language structures is Sentence Patterning Charts. (See Appendix: Activities that Support Reading & Writing Workshop, page 114.)

Supporting English Learners at Various English Proficiency Levels in Write-Alouds

WIDA
ELPA 21
ELPS/TELPAS

ENTERING	EMERGING	DEVELOPING/ EXPANDING	BRIDGING/ REACHING
1	2	3	4/5
Beginning	Intermediate	Advanced	Advanced High
• Model in small groups • Speak clearly and enunciate • Use slower speech • Allow primary language support • Use extensive visuals, illustrations, gestures, realia • Explicitly model thinking • Directly teach language structure and English language features	• Model in small groups • Speak clearly and enunciate • Use slower speech • Allow primary language support • Use extensive visuals, illustrations, gestures, realia • Explicitly model thinking • Directly teach language structure and English language features	• Explicitly model thinking • Directly teach language structure and English language features	• Explicitly model thinking • Directly teach language structure and English language features

Chapter 8

Shared Writing

"If we adults *listen* and **watch** closely, our children will invite us to share their worlds and their ways of living in the world."

– Lucy Calkins

WHAT IS SHARED WRITING?

In shared writing, teacher and students create a text together. Tompkins and Collom (2004) describe shared writing as "the bridge between more teacher-directed (modeled) writing and independent writing" (p. iii). There are two kinds of shared writing that we are going to explore in greater depth. The first type of shared writing is the **Language Experience Approach**, in which the students share an experience like a field trip or a science experiment, and then they dictate a story to the teacher (Ashton-Warner, 1963). The teacher writes the students' words (spelled correctly) on chart paper, stopping to ask them questions like what each word begins with or whether or not it should be capitalized. Students read the

writing piece chorally, then it is typically displayed on the wall or in the reading center for students to read on their own or in pairs. The second type of shared writing is **Interactive Writing,** in which students and teacher both do the writing (McKenzie, 1985). Students write the words they know, and the teacher writes unknown words. Typically, teachers use correction tape to correct words that are misspelled so the writing piece will serve as an example of correct writing.

WHAT SHARED WRITING IS NOT

Shared writing is not two students writing together or a written conversation. It is not writing answers to a worksheet with a partner, and it is not the pass-the-paper writing activity in which one student begins a story, then passes it on to the next student to continue, and so on. There is nothing wrong with these activities; they are just used for different purposes and are not what we are talking about when we say "shared writing."

THE BENEFITS OF SHARED WRITING FOR ENGLISH LEARNERS

Shared writing, including Interactive Writing and Language Experience Approach, is "an excellent technique for young ELLs who are at the beginning stage of writing and learning the alphabet, letter formation, and letter-sound correspondence" (Wright, 2015, p. 239). It is also helpful for older English learners who are newcomers. Shared writing lends itself well to differentiated instruction, so teachers are able to cater the lesson to English learners' needs (Tompkins & Collom, 2004). Necessary skills for individual learners, such as concepts about print, vocabulary, and phonics, can easily be integrated into each lesson. Just like with write-aloud, English learners are able to see a demonstration of the composing process. When students write on the chart paper in Interactive Writing, they are able to participate in the composing process as well, again forming the bridge between teacher-directed writing and independent writing. Tompkins and Collom (2004) recommend giving each student a small chalkboard or dry erase board to write the words along with the student writing on the chart paper. This allows students to practice forming words before they go on the chart paper and ensures all students are engaged.

As English learners come to school with differing levels of background knowledge and different levels of English proficiency, we should allow them to use pictures in and with their writing and ensure that we use a lot of high-frequency words used in instruction. Students should be given multiple opportunities to turn and talk to their neighbors about what they are hearing and seeing, and they should be given many opportunities to chorally read what the teacher and other students have written.

Gradual Release of Responsibility & Components of Literacy

I do	We do	You do
• Mini-Lesson	• Shared Reading	• Independent Reading
• Read-Aloud	• Guided Reading	• Independent Writing
• Write-Aloud	★Shared Writing	

explicit & modeled	structured & supported	automatic & natural

Similar to write-alouds, shared writing achieves the following:

- Makes thinking visible
- Serves as an example of English language structures
- Provides explicit instruction
- Supports language development
- Builds vocabulary
- Offers authentic grammar practice

ACCOMMODATING SHARED WRITING FOR ENGLISH LEARNERS

One way to support English learners with shared writing is the Cooperative Sentence Strip Paragraph (Project GLAD). The class is divided into groups of three or four, and each group gets a sentence strip and a marker. Students work together to create a sentence about a shared experience. After they have written it, each group places their sentence strip in the class pocket chart. The teacher guides the students through reading, revising, editing, and rereading the paragraph. Students make suggestions, and the teacher makes the changes on the chart. Sentences can be rearranged or combined. This activity has students using all four language domains: reading, writing, listening, and speaking. In addition, this technique builds on their funds of knowledge, the knowledge base that comes from their family and life experiences (González, Moll, & Amanti, 2005).

CLASSROOM SCENARIO

Ms. Montrose's class has just studied apples and the process of making applesauce. Each student was asked to bring an apple from home. When they got to school, students compared the apples they had brought on a "real graphs" created on butcher paper on the floor. They compared by size for one graph and color for another graph. Next, students and Ms. Montrose worked together to make applesauce. Afterward, she led students through the Language Experience Approach.

Ms. Montrose: *Ok, boys and girls, let's talk about the applesauce we just made. Turn to your shoulder partner and talk about what we did first.*

Students talk to their shoulder partners, and Ms. Montrose places a piece of chart paper in front of the class.

Ms. Montrose: *We are going to write a how-to paper about making applesauce. Ok, what was the first thing we did?*

She pulls a popsicle stick from a jar and looks at it. She does this to randomize the students she calls on.

Ms. Montrose: *Philip?*

Philip: *We peeled the apples.*

Ms. Montrose: *Let's start our how-to paper with that. How could we write that?*

Philip: *First, we peeled the apples.*

Ms. Montrose: *Oh, good! What sound do you hear at the beginning of "first," Philip?*

Philip: *F*

Ms. Montrose: *That's right, and what kind of letter should it be since it is at the beginning of the sentence, class?*

Class: *Capital.*

Ms. Montrose: *That's right!*

Ms. Montrose writes the word "First" at the top of the paper and adds a comma.

Ms. Montrose: *We put a comma here to show we pause. Think to yourself, how do you spell the word "we?"*

Ms. Montrose waits several seconds, then pulls another popsicle stick. This time it's Josie who is chosen.

Ms. Montrose: *Josie, how do you spell the word "we?"*

Josie: *w-e*

Ms. Montrose: *That's right, Josie!*

She writes "we" before posing another question.

Ms. Montrose: *Close your eyes and listen to this word. What do you hear at the beginning of "peeled"?*

She draws another popsicle stick and repeats the word.

Ms. Montrose: *Jaime, what do you hear at the beginning of "peeled?"*

Jaime: *P*

Ms. Montrose: *Absolutely!*

She writes "peeled."

Ms. Montrose: *And how do you spell "the," class?*

Class: *T-h-e*

Ms. Montrose: *Ok, now what do you hear at the beginning of "apples?"*

She pulls a popsicle stick.

Ms. Montrose: *Samantha?*

Samantha: *A*

Ms. Montrose: *Yes!*

She writes "apples" and pulls another popsicle stick.

Ms. Montrose: *Now, what do we need at the end of the sentence? Thomas?*

Thomas: *A period.*

Ms. Montrose: *You're right! A period.*

She adds a period.

Ms. Montrose: *Now, let's all read the first sentence together.*

Ms. Montrose points to each word as they read.

Ms. Montrose and class: *First, we peeled the apples.*

Ms. Montrose: *Now, turn to your shoulder partner and talk about what we did after we peeled the apples.*

Students talk to their shoulder partners, and Ms. Montrose proceeds in the same way for the rest of the how-to paper.

Each time a sentence was complete, she and the students read the sentence chorally. When the how-to paper was finished, Ms. Montrose and the students read the entire paper. Next, Ms. Montrose asked the students to return to their seats and begin writing their own how-to paper on a chosen topic. She gave the idea of writing about how to make a "real graph" if they wanted to use that topic. As the students wrote their how-to papers, Ms. Montrose walked around observing and conferring with students. She also placed the completed "How to Make Applesauce" story in the reading center for students to read in pairs.

Routman (2000) states, "Shared writing builds on what the teacher has already been modeling through write-aloud" (p. 37). According to Tompkins (2015), shared writing provides writing experiences for students that they are not yet able to do independently. Language Experience Approach and Interactive Writing allow students to practice writing before they are expected to write independently. Both approaches are based on the idea that children are able to read pieces of literature that they were involved in writing (Tompkins & Collom, 2004). In addition, students are able to see and hear the thought processes that go into writing, much like write-aloud. Routman (2005) stresses that shared writing is an excellent way to involve all students in oral and written language. The author states that shared writing helps to increase students' confidence in writing and enjoyment of the writing process, as the teacher serves as the "expert and scribe for her apprentices" (p. 83). As students dictate ideas, the teacher can expand on ideas and demonstrate complete sentences and organized writing.

Furthermore, shared writing can be a demonstration of good writing and is an excellent way to teach young students concepts about print (Routman, 2000). Shared writing is especially helpful for English learners and struggling readers, as it helps students hear and see the words as they are written.

Language Experience Approach Lesson Map

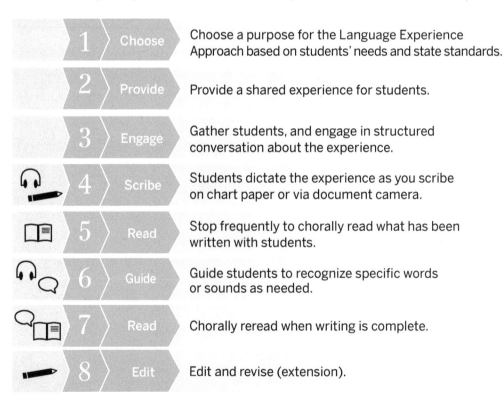

1	Choose	Choose a purpose for the Language Experience Approach based on students' needs and state standards.
2	Provide	Provide a shared experience for students.
3	Engage	Gather students, and engage in structured conversation about the experience.
4	Scribe	Students dictate the experience as you scribe on chart paper or via document camera.
5	Read	Stop frequently to chorally read what has been written with students.
6	Guide	Guide students to recognize specific words or sounds as needed.
7	Read	Chorally reread when writing is complete.
8	Edit	Edit and revise (extension).

Shared Writing Lesson Map

(Tompkins & Collom, 2004)*

1 Choose	Choose a purpose for shared writing based on students' needs and state standards.
2 Select	Select an engaging topic for shared writing.
3 Prepare	Gather students, and prepare to write on a whiteboard, document camera, or chart paper.
4 Collaborate	Collaborate with students to think of the first sentence.
5 Repeat	Individually repeat each word to be written.
6 Write	A student writes all or part of the current word.
7 Read	Students chorally read some of what has been written as you or the student points.
8 Repeat	Repeat the whole sentence together to refresh memory and begin writing the next sentence.

*Tompkins and Collom (2004) recommend using one color marker for words written by the students and another color for words written by the teacher.

Shared writing is especially helpful for English learners and struggling readers, as it helps students hear and see the words as they are written.

FAQ

What is the difference between the Language Experience Approach and Interactive Writing?

In the Language Experience Approach, students dictate to the teacher as both students and the teacher negotiate and agree upon a sentence. The teacher writes with correct spelling to serve as an example of conventional writing. In Interactive Writing, students and teacher share the pen. Students take turns writing what they are able to write, and teacher writes unknown words for students.

How long should a shared writing activity be?

A shared writing experience can be short and occur during one lesson, or it can last several weeks (Routman, 2000). The teacher can lead the class through the whole writing process as a shared writing to demonstrate the process. Teachers and students can even make a class book through shared writing.

At what grade levels would you do shared writing with students?

You can do shared writing with Kindergarten through high school students. For older students, shared writing can be an excellent way to introduce a new genre or technique or different writing styles. Routman (2000) explains, "This guided writing is the scaffold writers need in order to attempt a new genre or project" (p. 38).

What's the best way to ensure that English learners understand the content of the lesson and develop language?

Students that are acquiring English while simultaneously learning content benefit from explicit instruction with the use of content and language objectives. Language objectives that support the content, match the English language development or proficiency standards, and are measurable are most effective for English learners in our classrooms (Seidlitz & Perryman, 2011). Many teachers find that sharing content and language objectives with students at the beginning and end of the lesson helps students to narrow the goals for the instructional period and metacognitively think and connect to their learning. We can set students up for success by integrating academic language and vocabulary into the content and language objectives and by sharing the objectives with students (Echevarria & Graves, 2003).

Supporting English Learners at Various English Proficiency Levels in Shared Writing

ENTERING	EMERGING	DEVELOPING/ EXPANDING	BRIDGING/ REACHING
1	2	3	4/5
Beginning	Intermediate	Advanced	Advanced High
• Model in small groups • Provide sentence in stems or frames • Allow primary language support • Use extensive visuals, illustrations, gestures, realia • Provide opportunities for peer collaboration • Explicitly model thinking • Directly teach language structure and English language features	• Model in small groups • Provide sentence in stems or frames • Allow primary language support • Use extensive visuals, illustrations, gestures, realia • Provide opportunities for peer collaboration • Explicitly model thinking • Directly teach language structure and English language features	• Offer complex sentence frames • Provide opportunities for peer collaboration • Explicitly model thinking • Directly teach language structure and English language features	• Offer complex sentence frames • Provide opportunities for peer collaboration • Explicitly model thinking • Directly teach language structure and English language features

Chapter 9
Independent Writing

"Either write something worth reading or do something worth writing."

– Benjamin Franklin

WHAT IS INDEPENDENT WRITING?

In independent writing, students use the writing process to create independent text on a topic of choice. The writing process includes pre-writing, drafting, revising, editing, publishing, and sharing. While students work through the writing process, the teacher confers with individual students or students confer with one another. Many teachers choose to have students write in a daily Writing Workshop.

THE WRITING PROCESS LOOKS LIKE THIS:

Pre-writing: Students make a plan for what they are going to write. Typically, students brainstorm and create some type of graphic organizer to record their thoughts.

Drafting: Students write freely and get their thoughts down on paper. Teachers usually tell

students not to worry about correct spelling at this time, as they will be able to go back and fix their work later.

Revising: Students look back over their papers and move things around, change wording, and ensure what they have written makes sense to readers. Typically, a teacher will confer with the student before revisions begin. Many times, students will engage in peer conferences before this step as well.

Editing: Students look at their work again and make corrections in spelling and punctuation. Students will usually have a teacher or peer conference before this step as well.

Publishing: Students decide how they want their finished products to look. This may be in the form of a paper, a book, a shape book, a poster, a letter, or a variety of other forms. Students make sure to use their best handwriting and make all corrections. They may also use the computer to rewrite their pieces.

Sharing: Students share their writing in many different ways. In a typical classroom, students volunteer to share their works at the end of Writing Workshop time while sitting in the author's chair. Many schools have an Authors' Day during which students share what they have written with parents, classmates, and visitors to the school.

Gradual Release of Responsibility & Components of Literacy

I do	We do	You do
• Mini-Lesson	• Shared Reading	• Independent Reading
• Read-Aloud	• Guided Reading	★Independent Writing
• Write-Aloud	• Shared Writing	

explicit & modeled	structured & supported	automatic & natural

WHAT INDEPENDENT WRITING IS NOT

Independent writing is not writing to a prompt. Students should have a choice of what to write about. Independent writing is also not expected to be perfect, grammatically correct writing during the drafting step. Just like basketball, dance, or piano, students must practice writing by actually writing in order to become proficient at it. Independent writing provides this practice for students.

THE BENEFITS OF INDEPENDENT WRITING FOR ENGLISH LEARNERS

In independent writing, students are able to write at their own pace and their own level about something they know about. Gail Tompkins, author of *Literacy in the Early Grades: A Successful Start for PreK-4 Readers and Writers*, provides helpful guidance for setting up independent writing for English learners. According to Tompkins (2015), "English learners can become good writers when their teacher sets high expectations, teaches them how to write, and involves them in daily writing activities" (p. 329).

It is also beneficial for English learners to write on familiar topics. Tompkins (2015) recommends that students first write about their families and things in their everyday lives. Eventually, they can move into writing about topics they are studying in school and books they have read. Teachers can help students write independently by providing sentence stems and graphic organizers for them.

Teachers can determine the needs of English learners by conferring with them and using information from the conferences to form strategy groups for those with similar needs. It is important to focus on a student's content rather than mechanics during conference time. Then the teacher can scaffold the student through the revision and editing processes.

Talk is important for all students as they go through the writing process, but it is especially important for English learners to have conversations about their writing (Tompkins, 2015). Teachers can provide a word bank and sentence stems to make the process easier for students. In addition, English learners often find that pattern books and predictable books can serve as models for their writing. Tompkins also reminds us that the Language Experience Approach and Interactive Writing (see p. 94-95) are valuable to use as models with English learners as they begin to write using the writing process.

ACCOMMODATING INDEPENDENT WRITING FOR ENGLISH LEARNERS

Since English learners have different levels of background knowledge and language proficiency, it is important for them to write using pictures or in their native language if need be.

For example, one student in my first grade class drew pictures with a few one- to two-letter labels and told stories orally in English for his writing. As he gradually became more proficient, he included more words and fewer pictures in his writing.

— Melinda

Honigsfeld (2019) reminds us that English fluency is not a prerequisite for writing and that we cannot wait for students to fully develop English language proficiency to begin to write. However, it is important for teachers to understand that independent writing can be a confusing block of time for English learners if used without accommodation, scaffolds, and structures to support students at varying proficiency levels. Students who need linguistic support may not be able to write without specific scaffolds. Knowing your students' language levels well will help you determine which scaffolds they need and when to release them.
Here are a few you can try:

- Meet frequently with students one-on-one or in small groups.
- Teach students to use graphic organizers for planning.
- Allow drawing and labeling.
- Allow primary language support and writing in primary language.
- Provide opportunities to talk with a peer before, during, and after the writing process.
- Give students attainable targets of writing or exemplars.
- Provide students with frequent feedback.
- Provide sentence stems for students.
- Provide scaffolded paragraph frames for students.

CLASSROOM SCENARIO

Ms. Dunlavy has just finished a mini-lesson on writing strong introductions. This mini-lesson topic seemed to be needed by the whole class. As they go back to their seats to write on their own, she reminds them that they can try writing an interesting introduction for their pieces.

While students are writing, Ms. Dunlavy wheels around in her rolling chair and visits with individual students privately. As she stops by Fatima's desk, Fatima excitedly turns to her teacher.

Fatima: *Listen to my introduction!*

Ms. Dunlavy listens as Fatima reads.

Ms. Dunlavy: *Wow, Fatima! That is really a strong introduction.*

She wheels up to Esteban and notices that he doesn't have anything written on his paper.

Ms. Dunlavy: *Hi, Esteban! How's it going? Hmmm, do you have any ideas about what you would like to write?*

Esteban shrugs with wide eyes.

Ms. Dunlavy: *What is something you love? What do you know a lot about?*

She places her paper where Esteban can see it. She draws a heart and writes the words "I like."

Ms. Dunlavy: *Hmmm, what do I like? Let's see. I like books.*

She writes "books" next to "I like." She draws a picture of a book, and she reads, "I like books."

Ms. Dunlavy: *What else do I like? Oh, I like dogs.*

She writes, "I like dogs," and draws a picture of a dog next to it. She gives a few more examples.

Ms. Dunlavy: *Esteban, what do you like?*

She writes, "I like_____." Together they brainstorm a list of things Esteban can write about. Ms. Dunlavy asks him to pick a topic and write about it in either English or Spanish.

Ms. Dunlavy moves on to the next student. Esteban is at the beginner proficiency level. While most students in the class are working on strong introductions, he is not ready to work on a strong beginning yet. He is, however, at the point where he is ready to choose a topic and write. As Ms. Dunlavy confers with students, she is able to tailor instruction to meet them where they are and to help them build upon their strengths.

WHAT THE EXPERTS SAY

Murray (1972) describes writing as a process and emphasizes the need for teachers to focus on the process of writing rather than the finished product. According to Flower and Hayes (1986), the writing process is made up of the following components: planning, translating, and reviewing.

All students, including very young children and English learners, can learn to think about what they want to write and put their words down on paper using the writing process (Tompkins, 2015). The writing process is broken down into achievable steps, but the steps are fluid and do not always happen in the same order. Each writer spends different amounts of time in each of these steps, with the most amount of time typically spent prewriting (Murray, 1972).

One way to support students in the writing process is by dedicating regular class time to Writing Workshop (Fletcher & Portalupi, 2007). During Writing Workshop time, the classroom becomes a community of writers guided by the teacher (Tompkins, 2015). Students are able to work at their own levels and pace so teachers can easily differentiate instruction through mini-lessons and conferences.

The three basic needs of writers, according to Nancie Atwell's teacher friend and writing guru, Mary Ellen Giacobbe, are time, ownership, and response (Atwell, 1987). Similarly, Fu and Lamme (2002) recognize time, choice, and response as writers' fundamental needs. Graves (1994) identifies the optimal conditions for writing as time, choice, response, demonstration, expectation, room structure, and evaluation. Writers need a sustained time every day during which they can practice orchestrating their thinking and all they know about the composing process.

Students should be able to choose their own writing topics so they will be interested and engaged and feel ownership over their writing (Tompkins, 2015). It is beneficial for students to write about what they know about.

In addition, students should be given the opportunity to receive responses to their writing in the form of teacher conferences, peer conferences, and feedback from peers during author's chair time. Graves stresses that "students need to hear the responses of others to their writing, to discover what they do or do not understand" (p. 108). The author also emphasizes the importance of students seeing a demonstration of writers' craft and teachers' high expectations of all student writers. Furthermore, the classroom environment should be conducive to writing and include predictable times during which students can write. Finally, students must learn to evaluate their own writing and know when to add, revise, or delete something. The teacher's role is to coordinate all of these conditions to ensure students learn what it is to be a writer. Writing Workshop supports writers and their needs.

The connection between reading and writing cannot be understated, as researchers have established a "strong relationship between ELLs' reading ability and their writing ability in English" (Wright, 2015, p. 226). As students gain vocabulary and grammar structures from reading, they begin to apply them in their writing. The more English learners read, the more they write, and the better they become at writing.

Independent Writing Lesson Map

1	Choose	Choose a purpose for Independent Writing based on students' needs and state standards.
2	Select	Have students choose topics for writing.
3	Brainstorm	Have students brainstorm using graphic organizers for pre-writing.
4	Compose	Have students compose their writing pieces without attention to spelling and punctuation.
5	Confer	Confer with students about their first drafts.
6	Revise & Edit	Help students determine revisions and edits to be made in their writing pieces.
7	Publish	Guide students to publish their writing pieces.
8	Share	Provide an opportunity for students to share writing though Author's Chair or Authors' Day.

FAQ

What if my district requires we do writing prompts in preparation for the state test?

Tompkins (2015) states that "good writing instruction is the best way to prepare children for on-demand writing assessments" (p. 332). At the same time, students need to know how to write specifically for the writing test. We recommend that teachers use writing prompts at a separate time from Writing Workshop. If the district allows, we believe it is best to interrupt the writing process a few weeks before the state test in order to practice specifically for the test. Students can practice reading and responding to prompts. They must learn that there will be a time restriction and that they may have to write about something they are not interested in. Teachers can stress to students that this is a specific type of writing done for the test. After the test, students can go back to the writing process and Writing Workshop. Donalyn Miller (2009) teaches test taking as a genre. She states,

"Any activity that replaces extensive reading, writing, and discourse in the classroom needs to be better than the activity it replaces..."

How much of a student's spelling should I correct?

According to Tompkins (2015), "When children begin writing, teachers accept their work as it's written and focus on the message. Then as children gain experience with writing, teachers encourage them to fix more and more of their errors" (p. 322). We encourage teachers to keep track of students' word and spelling knowledge and hold them accountable according to their development as writers.

What do I tell a parent about invented spelling?

We encourage teachers to let parents know about the value of invented spelling. Students must approximate the spelling of words using their knowledge of hearing and recording sounds in words (Clay, 1993). Invented spelling is like a window into a child's brain to see what they are thinking as they are writing their own versions of words. They gradually reach the point at which they understand how to record sounds with letters, and they learn the various spelling patterns through trial and error and through word work and systematic instruction provided by the teacher.

How does independent writing fit in with Writing Workshop?

Tasha Tropp Laman, author of *From Ideas to Words*, reminds us that "no one learns without support, practice, guidance, and feedback" (p. 4). She goes on to say that Writing Workshop can provide English learners with just that. It also gives teachers the ability to pay close attention to students' needs "in order to guide their current and future instruction" (p. 5).

How often should we do Writing Workshop?

We recommend implementing Writing Workshop every day, if possible. Ideally, Writing Workshop should last about 60 minutes. One of the needs of writers identified by Atwell (1998) is time. Children should have a daily sustained time to practice writing in order to become proficient.

Here is an example of what Writing Workshop could look like:

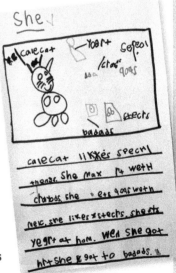

Mini-lesson: Teacher addresses specific skills based upon students' writing. The mini-lesson can be a write-aloud, or it can include literature read as an example of the author's style.

Writing time: Students write independently using the writing process while the teacher gathers students for conferences. The teacher may also visit students at their desks for a roving conference. Peer conferences can also happen during this time.

Sharing time: Students share their writing pieces with partners or with the whole group.

(Tompkins, 2015; Cooper, 2000; Atwell, 1998).

What do I do while students write independently?

Independent writing time gives you the freedom to move about your classroom and meet with individual students and small groups. There are a few options for teachers while students write independently. Most importantly, teachers give students feedback during the writing process through conferences or through groups. Simply providing time and choice for writing will not guarantee that students will become stronger writers. See "Activities that Support Independent Writing" (p. 116-117) for more information about conferring with writers and gathering students in strategy groups.

How can I support English learners who seem to struggle during independent writing time?

Keeping an eye on English learners during independent writing time is very important. Without enough structure and support, some English learners may find this time confusing and frustrating.

One way to support ELs at the beginner levels of English proficiency is to provide visuals for writing. See Appendix: Activities that Support Reading & Writing Workshop, specifically the section Picture Word Inductive Model on p.125.

Supporting English Learners at Various
English Proficiency Levels in Independent Writing

ENTERING	EMERGING	DEVELOPING/ EXPANDING	BRIDGING/ REACHING
1	2	3	4/5
Beginning	Intermediate	Advanced	Advanced High
• Allow primary language support and writing in primary language • Allow drawing and labeling • Provide opportunities for peer collaboration before, during, and after writing • Provide sentence stems and/or paragraph frames • Teach the use of graphic organizers • Meet in small groups and confer frequently • Provide exemplar texts	• Model in small groups • Provide sentences with stems or frames • Allow primary language support • Use extensive visuals, illustrations, gestures, realia • Provide opportunities for peer collaboration • Explicitly model thinking • Directly teach language structure and English language features • Provide exemplar texts	• Offer complex sentence frames • Provide opportunities for peer collaboration • Explicitly model thinking • Directly teach language structure and English language features • Provide exemplar texts	• Offer complex sentence frames • Provide opportunities for peer collaboration • Explicitly model thinking • Directly teach language structure and English language features • Provide exemplar texts

APPENDIX I

Activities that Support Reading & Writing Workshop

QSSSA

WHEN TO USE: Mini-Lesson & Read-Aloud

QSSSA is an instructional technique that increases total participation (Seidlitz & Perryman, 2011). Rather than the teacher asking a question and calling on one or two students to answer, QSSSA provides an opportunity for all students to engage in thinking, listening, and speaking.

STEPS:

1. Pose an open-ended **question** to the class.

2. Ask students to give a **signal** (stand up, close your book, hands on your hips, etc.) when they have an answer.

3. Provide students with a sentence **stem** to support speaking in complete sentences.

4. Pair or group students, and model expectations for **sharing** their responses. For example, "The student with the most buttons will share first." Have partners practice listening by responding with one of these stems before sharing their own ideas. "What I heard you say was that…" or "Can you explain more about…"

5. Finally, **assess** students' comprehension by either randomly calling on a few students or having all students write tickets out. This step holds all students accountable for the learning.

Q-S-S-S-A
Q-Question: Pose an open-ended, engaging question.
S-Signal: Ask student to show a signal when they are prepared to answer the question.
S-Stem: Provide a sentence frame or starter.
S-Share: Student share with a partner or group.
A-Assess: Randomly select a few students to share with the whole group.

Reader's Theater

WHEN TO USE:
Shared Reading

Reader's theater is character-
ized as text that is developed
into a play (Young & Rasinski,
2009). Students and the teacher
work together to take a familiar
reading and create a dialogue.
Reader's theater offers students
opportunities to increase fluency and practice oral reading.

STEPS:

1. Select a text to transform into a reader's theater.

2. Model how to choose part of the text for the reader's theater.

3. Guide students through the process of turning parts of the text into dialogue.

4. Encourage students to create props if necessary.

5. Divide the narration and dialogue among the students.

6. Provide rehearsal time. This time is for students to practice fluency and expression but not to memorize their parts.

7. Students either perform for a live audience of peers (younger or older) or record their reader's theater on a digital platform and share broadly.

Echo Reading

WHEN TO USE:
Shared Reading

Echo reading supports both early
readers and English learners. Because
the teacher models the reading first, all
students hear what the words should
sound like. The teacher sets an example. When students echo the sentence
back in unison, the affective filter is
lowered. Students do not feel singled
out to read in front of the group, nor do
they feel the pressure of reading every
word. Some students may not read each
word during the echo because they
need more space to listen to their peer
models. Echo reading provides students
with a safe learning environment to
practice reading in a community of
readers.

STEPS:

1. Display the text for all students to see.

2. Read a word or sentence (while tracking the print), and invite students to repeat or echo.

3. Have the students echo your words, tone, and expression as they read.

Example

Teacher: Readers, first I'll read, and then you read after me. Let's try. "There will be times when you walk into a room and no one there is quite like you."

Students: "There will be times when you walk into a room and no one there is quite like you."

Activities

Choral Reading

WHEN TO USE:
Shared Reading

Choral reading, like echo reading, supports both early readers and English learners. However, during choral reading, everyone reads in unison (even the teacher). This level of support is slightly less than the support given during echo reading. Students still benefit from a safe, risk-free reading environment. As opposed to the traditional method of calling on one student at a time to read, choral reading does not put students on the spot or raise anxiety.

STEPS:

1. Display the text for all students to see.

2. Read in unison with the students while tracking print.

Conferring With Readers/Writers

WHEN TO USE:
Independent Reading and Writing

Conferring, simply put, is holding an individual conversation about reading or writing with a student. Conferences with students help build relationships and trust. They implicitly tell students that you care about them as readers or writers, care about their interests, and are invested in their growth. Conferring with students allows for monitoring academic and linguistic progress. Conferences are quick, lasting just three to five minutes.

STEPS:

1. Begin by observing the class as a whole during independent reading/writing.

2. Take anecdotal notes of your observations. What are students doing? What behaviors do they exhibit as readers/writers?

3. Develop a plan for meeting with each student throughout the week during independent reading/writing. Perhaps meet with three to five students daily.

4. When sitting down next to a learner, begin with a warm greeting, such as, "Hi Diego. How's that book coming along? Do you like it?" Listen, and take anecdotal notes that will help guide your instruction for this student. Ask probing questions, listen to the students read a page, compliment them on a strategy they used, and if needed, coach them on a skill that can help them grow as readers.

5. After conferring with many students throughout the week, analyze the notes and look for trends. If there is a group with a similar need, gather them for a strategy lesson (see "strategy groups" on pg. 117).

Strategy Groups

WHEN TO USE:
Independent Reading and Writing

Strategy groups are powerful, small group lessons specifically tailored to meet certain students' reading or writing needs. They are similar to guided reading groups but differ in some distinct ways. Rather than gathering students with comparable reading levels, they gather students who have similar goals in reading or writing. For that reason, these groups are flexible. Strategy groups last about 15 minutes as the remainder of the class reads or writes independently.

Let's say, for example, that as you observe students as readers, you notice that four of them exhibit a similar reading need. They are all reading word for word and not attending to punctuation. The learning goal is for them to read with more fluency and prosody in an effort to comprehend text, but the rest of the class does not need this type of support. Instead of going to each of these students one at a time, it would be more efficient to gather them in a group and hold a quick mini-lesson to support them.

As the rest of the class reads independently, gather these four students, asking them to bring along the book they are reading currently. The mini-lesson is quick and involves direct teaching and active participation. You want students to know what they are there to learn, and you want them to walk away with a new strategy in their tool belts.

Model using a mentor text, and then ask them to try the strategy in the books they brought with them. Support the students as they give it a try, then end the lesson with a reminder of how they can use this strategy in their everyday reading lives.

STEPS:

1. Observe the students as readers/writers during independent reading/writing and during one-on-one conferences. Take anecdotal notes.

2. Analyze the anecdotal notes, and build groups based on needs. For example, if you notice that four students are reading through punctuation, this might be a group.

3. During independent reading/writing, gather the small group of students for a strategy lesson based on your observation. The remainder of the class will continue to read/write independently.

4. Begin the lesson with a quick, explicit lesson of a strategy to support the students' goal.

5. Provide students with time to practice the new strategy with your support, immediate feedback, and assistance.

Guided Reading

WHEN TO USE: Independent Reading

(For more on guided reading, see Chapter 5 on pages 62-75)

Partner Reading

WHEN TO USE:
Independent Reading

Providing opportunities for students to pair up and read with a peer "builds engagement in literacy" (Ferlazzo & Sypnieski, 2018). This approach allows for listening, speaking, and reading practice in a safe setting. Though it may not seem as if partner reading is independent reading, students are reading on their own but with other students at their sides. Some teachers pair students who are at similar reading levels for partner reading. The purpose of partner reading is for students to have a peer they can discuss their books with in order to dig deeper into their comprehension.

When establishing partnerships with your students, be clear about the expectations. Modeling what partner reading looks and sounds like will help set students up for success. Unstructured partner reading can lead to frustration for some students. English learners may benefit from sentence starters that they can have available during partner reading. For example, "You read about…" "The main idea was…" "I'm wondering about…" "Can you reread…"

STEPS:

1. Intentionally pair students, keeping literacy and language needs in mind.

2. Model expectations such as how students will sit, who will read first, and what listeners will do.

3. Provide students with reader and listener roles. For example, as the reader reads a paragraph, the listener will listen and summarize what the reader said using words such as, "One important thing you read was…"

4. Students switch roles as directed, after paragraphs, chapters, or pages.

Hearing and Recording Sounds in Words (Elkonin Boxes)

WHEN TO USE: Independent Reading and Writing

This activity is done using small plastic discs.

STEPS:

1. Draw a box on the page for each sound in a word ("cat," for example).

2. Have the student articulate the word slowly, stretching out the sounds ("caaaaaat").

3. Show the child how to push the discs into the boxes each time a sound is heard. After saying the word slowly and pushing the discs a couple of times, ask the student, "What did you hear?" "How will you write it?" and "Where will you put it?"

4. Have the student write the letters in each box to write the word (c-a-t), then read the word again. It is a good idea to have the student locate the word in a book after it is written to help make a connection between reading and writing (Clay, 1993; Hoyt, 2000; Reutzel & Cooter, 2003; McGee & Richgels, 2008; Tompkins, 2014).

Making and Breaking Words

WHEN TO USE:
Guided Reading

Making and breaking words comes directly from Reading Recovery (Clay, 1993). Making and breaking helps a student to see how words work and how you can read or write a new word by looking at and thinking about a known word.

STEPS:

1. Give the student enough magnetic letters to make a word they know, and ask them to make the word.

2. Ask the student to read the word. Next, show the child that another word can be made by changing one letter in the word.

3. Have the student make the new word and read it out loud.

4. Continue showing the student other letters that can replace the changed letter. For example, if the child makes "look," change it to "book," "hook," "cook," "took," etc.

5. Have the student locate the known word in a book after the activity to link the strategy back to the text.

Analogies

WHEN TO USE:
Guided Reading and Independent Writing

Analogies can be pulled from a child's reading or writing (Clay, 1993). Making analogies is very similar to making and breaking words, but they are written. This strategy helps children read and spell unknown words using words they already know.

STEPS:

1. For an analogy, ask the student to write a known word, such as "like."

2. After the student writes "like," say, "If you can write 'like,' you can also write 'bike.' If you can write 'bike,' you can also write 'hike,'" etc.

3. Go back and have the student find the known word in the text or in the student's own writing.

My Pile/Your Pile

WHEN TO USE: Guided Reading

In my pile/your pile, the teacher writes down some words the student already knows on index cards, then adds a few words the student is trying to learn (Clay, 1993). The object is for the student to read the stack of cards as quickly as possible. New words can be added to the stack as the student masters more and more words. My pile/your pile helps with instant recognition of sight words, which may be more difficult for English learners because many sight words are abstract and others may violate known spelling rules (Thompkins, 2014). Starting with known words and adding a few new words at a time helps students experience success with this activity.

STEPS:

1. Hold up the cards flashcard style, and ask the student to read the words.

2. If the word is read correctly, put it in the student's pile.

3. If not, put it in your pile, and give the student another chance to read and practice the word.

Chunks

WHEN TO USE: Guided Reading and Independent Reading

If students can learn "chunks" or parts of words that are often found together, they can look for those parts in unknown words they are trying to read (Clay, 1993; Fox, 2004). For instance, students can read "farmer" if they know "ar," "er," "arm," or "farm."

STEPS:

1. Prompt the child to use this strategy by saying, "Find a part you know," or "Can you find a little word in that big word?"

2. Have children practice this strategy by doing a word sort, placing all the words that contain a certain chunk in a specific pile.

3. For another way to practice the use of the chunk strategy, have children underline chunks found in words they are trying to read (Bear, Invernizzi, Templeton, & Johnston, 2008).

Strategy Tents

WHEN TO USE:
Guided Reading and
Independent Reading

Strategy tents are made by folding a large index card or piece of tag board to make a "tent" that will stand on the students' desks. The children can keep their strategy tents on their desks to refer to as they are reading, so they can remember the strategies that help them read. A variation is to include this information on a bookmark instead. These are also referred to as "Fix It!" Bookmarks (Hoyt, 2000).

STEPS:

1. Begin by brainstorming with students things they can do to help themselves read.

2. Encourage students to write those strategies on their own strategy tents.

3. Have the students add pictures to help them remember the strategies if they wish.

Strategies that might be included on the tent:

- Re-read
- Check the picture
- Think about what makes sense
- Look for a little word in the big word
- Start the word and read across it
- Try the word and read on

Beginning-Middle-End: Finding Phonemes in Sound Boxes

WHEN TO USE:
Guided Reading

Like hearing and recording sounds in words, or Elkonin Boxes, this activity shows how words are made up of sounds and represented by letters. Students can take turns coming up to find each sound or letter and name the letter. The word can then be read together, then students can locate the word in a book to tie it back to the context of literature (Bear, Invernizzi, Templeton, & Johnston, 2004).

STEPS:

1. First, make a foldable with three pockets to put letter cards in.

2. Next, label the pockets with "beginning, middle, end" and place letter cards in the pockets (turned backward so that the students cannot see them) to spell a familiar three-letter word.

3. Next, sing the following song to the tune of "Are You Sleeping, Brother John?"
   Beginning, middle, end; beginning, middle, end
   Where is the sound? Where is the sound?
   Where's the /s/ in sun? Where's the /s/ in sun?
   Let's find out! Let's find out!

4. Finally, have the students take turns turning the letters over to reveal the sounds.

5. Read the sounds together with the students.

Word Sorts

WHEN TO USE: Guided Reading

Word sorts can use words that come from the students' reading and writing. Words can be sorted by beginning letters, beginning consonant clusters, or medial vowels, for example.

STEPS:

1. Write words on small cards, making sure that at least one word is a well-known word.

2. Model the sorting process, placing a well-known word at the top of the column.

3. Next, read each word and talk about a particular characteristic, such as the vowel sound you hear in the word, stating that students will now look for other words with that same characteristic.

4. Guide students through the word sort the first time, talking about why words go in each column.

5. Next, have students practice the sort with the teacher or in groups, then individually (Bear, Invernizzi, Templeton, & Johnston, 2004).

Sample Word Sort

not let shop
leg top bed sock
red hot peg

Language Experience Approach

WHEN TO USE:
Shared Writing

The Language Experience Approach is a teaching technique that builds on students' own vocabulary, experiences, and language patterns to strengthen their reading and writing in an authentic, meaningful way (Ashton-Warner, 1963).

STEPS:

1. Facilitate a class discussion over a shared experience such as a field trip, experiment, movie, book, etc.

2. Have students work in groups or pairs to make sentences related to the experience.

3. Have them dictate the sentences as you scribe them on chart paper or under a document camera for all to see.

4. Have the class read the sentences in unison as they are written.

5. Guide students in editing and revising the piece of writing.

Sentence Patterning Chart

WHEN TO USE:
Write-Aloud
Shared Writing

Sentence patterning charts are cocreated charts that model language structures and build vocabulary. Creating charts with students helps them practice language structures authentically and in a low-risk environment. This technique can be implemented as a whole group or in small groups.

STEPS:

1. Select a topic or theme that is relevant and compelling to students. Perhaps students are writing "All About ___" books during independent writing time. Share a visual related to the theme, and label it as a group. The labeled visual serves as a word bank.

2. Make a chart with two to three columns (e.g., can, have, are).

3. Under each column, brainstorm words together. (See example below).

4. Chorally read each column after completing it.

5. Model for students how to use the labeled picture and the chart to build sentences aloud.

6. Provide students time to practice their own sentences with partners.

DOGS

ARE	HAVE	CAN
ANIMALS	FOUR LEGS	BARK
MAMMALS	PAWS	RUN
CUTE	SNOUT	JUMP
FUN	SHARP TEETH	PLAY

Picture Word Inductive Model

WHEN TO USE:
Independent Writing
Shared Writing

The Picture Word Inductive Model (PWIM) provides ELs with a word bank and sentence stems for writing (Calhoun, 1999). This engaging method builds on students' background and prior knowledge, leveraging what they already know. The PWIM is a scaffold for writers who need additional support.

STEPS:

1. Select an engaging picture and share it with the small group or class.

2. Provide students with time to independently brainstorm as many words as they can about the visual.

3. Bring the group together in close proximity. Label the visuals as a group.

4. Guide students in building sentences using the labels.
   a. I see...
   b. There are...
   c. The ___ has...

5. Let students practice verbally sharing sentences with a partner.

6. Model how to write a paragraph using the labeled visual.

Picture Word Inductive Model

1. Select relevant/compelling picture and project it.

2. Label with students.

3. Develop sentences.

4. Build paragraphs.

I see.....

The _____ has ____ and a_____.

I can infer that.... because.....

APPENDIX II

The Role of Phonics

There is no question about it: Phonics play an important role in literacy, especially in the primary grades and when teaching English learners whose home languages are not Latin based. Take for example Li, a second grade student from China. Li is literate in Chinese. He can read, write, listen, and speak proficiently, as a child his age should, in his primary language. Now as a second grade student in the United States, Li must learn a new alphabet that is very different from the characters that he is used to reading. He will need to learn the letters and the sounds in order to read and write in English, and he'll also need to learn to read from left to right instead of right to left.

Phonics can be defined as "the relationships between phonology, the sounds in speech, and orthography, the spelling system" (Tompkins, 2015, p. 115). When students understand that speech is made up of sounds and they can manipulate those sounds within a word, they have achieved phonemic awareness. When students then begin to associate those sounds with letters and are able to record sounds in words, they are using phonics. They also use phonics when they recognize individual letters and the sounds they make and when they read across a word from left to right to put those sounds together.

Tompkins (2015) emphasizes that phonics instruction should focus on patterns of letters because in English, there is no one-to-one correspondence between letters and sounds. Letters are pronounced differently according to their position in a word, the other letters adjacent to them, and in many cases the origin of the word itself. Some consonants can make more than one sound (eg., c and g), and every vowel makes at least two different sounds.

During shared reading, teachers can point out specific sounds found in words. In Write-Aloud and shared writing exercises, teachers can emphasize the sounds of each letter they are using and clarify which sounds go together in specific words. This example points to the importance of students learning to identify sounds in words (phonemic awareness) before they are able to record those sounds with written letters.

Teaching students the idea of onset and rime helps them to learn how to think about word families. The onset is the consonant at the beginning of a one-syllable word (if any), and the rime includes all the letters that follow the consonant. For example, in the word cat, /c/ is the onset, and /at/ is the rime. Word families can be taught using magnetic letters with Making and Breaking words (see p. 120) or in writing with Analogies (see p. 120). Words found in students' own writing can also lead to the study of word families. For instance, if a student has written the word "day," the teacher can have her write the word "day" on a practice piece of paper, then say, "If you can write 'day,' you can also write 'way'" and so on. As students study word families, it is helpful to make charts of the word families and hang them around the classroom for reference.

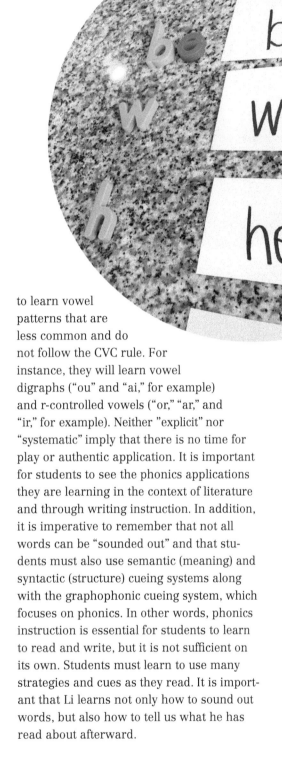

In the early grades, phonics can be taught to the whole group since all students will need the same or similar instruction. In later years, it may best to deliver phonics instruction through small groups or individually for students who missed the instructions initially, like Li for instance, who came to America when he was only in the second grade. According to the International Literacy Association (2019), "Teaching students the basic letter-sound combinations gives them access to sounding out approximately 84 percent of words in English print." Not only will students need to know how to read the words, but they will also need to understand the meanings of the words.

Phonics instruction that is explicit and systematic has been proven to be effective for students. "Explicit" means developing intentional plans for introducing letter-sound relationships, including word families. "Systematic" means following a scope and sequence that moves from simple to complex. This ensures that skills are not missed. Typically, teachers introduce consonants first, then short vowels, so students are able to write simple CVC words like "cat," "bed," and "sit." Afterward, students can learn digraphs and blends to write words like "ship," "frog," and "chop" (Tompkins, 2015).

After students have had more exposure to books and other print materials, they will begin to recognize many sight words and start to learn vowel patterns that are less common and do not follow the CVC rule. For instance, they will learn vowel digraphs ("ou" and "ai," for example) and r-controlled vowels ("or," "ar," and "ir," for example). Neither "explicit" nor "systematic" imply that there is no time for play or authentic application. It is important for students to see the phonics applications they are learning in the context of literature and through writing instruction. In addition, it is imperative to remember that not all words can be "sounded out" and that students must also use semantic (meaning) and syntactic (structure) cueing systems along with the graphophonic cueing system, which focuses on phonics. In other words, phonics instruction is essential for students to learn to read and write, but it is not sufficient on its own. Students must learn to use many strategies and cues as they read. It is important that Li learns not only how to sound out words, but also how to tell us what he has read about afterward.

Culturally Inclusive Book List

Title	Author	Themes	Culture
The Day You Begin	Jacqueline Woodson	Being new, trying something new	Various
Wilma Unlimited	Kathleen Krull	Determination, persistence, overcoming adversity	African American
Shaking Things Up	Susan Hood	Extraordinary women	Various
Under My Hijab	Hena Khan	Muslim tradition	Muslim tradition
The Royal Bee	Francis Park & Ginger Park	Education, determination	Korean
The Name Jar	Yangsook Choi	Being new, identity, names	Korean
Drum Dream Girl	Margarita Engle	Breaking stereotypes, dreams	Cuban
Too Many Tamales	Gary Soto	Tradition	Hispanic
Ruby's Wish	Shirin Yim Bridges	Education, determination	Chinese
This Is How We Do It	Matt Lamothe	Diversity	Various
All Are Welcome	Alexandra Penfold	Diversity	Various
The Invisible Boy	Trudy Ludwig	Inclusion, being different, being new	Various
Islandborn	Junot Díaz	New world, identity, imagination, family, belonging	Various
Salam Alaikum	Harris J	Greetings, peace, love, happiness	Muslim
Joseph's Big Ride	Terry Farish	Immigrant, new friendships, refugee	South Sudan
The Lotus Seed	Sherry Garland	Roots, memories, history	Vietnamese
Carmela Full of Wishes	Matt de la Peña	Dreams, hopes	Hispanic
Rainbow Weaver	Linda Elovitz	Traditions	Guatemalan
Same, Same but Different	Jenny Sue Kostecki-Shaw	Diversity, differences	Indian
The Empty Pot	Demi	Integrity, honesty	Chinese
Love	Matt de la Peña	Bonds of love	Various

Title	Author	Themes	Culture
Alma and How She Got Her Name	Juana Martinez-Neal	Identity, names	Hispanic
Big Red Lollipop	Rukhsana Khan	Traditions	Middle Eastern
The Sandwich Swap	Queen Rania al Abdullah	Diversity, friendships	All
Esperanza Rising	Pam Muñoz Ryan	Immigrants, farm workers	Mexican American
The Color of Us	Karen Katz	Diversity	All
Flossie and the Fox	Patricia C. McKissack	Tradition	African American
The Other Side	Jacquelyn Woodson	Diversity	All
Sister Anne's Hands	Marybeth Lorbiecki	Diversity	All
Separate is Never Equal: Sylvia Mendez and her Family's Fight for Desegregation	Duncan Tonatiuh	Desegregation	Hispanic
The Colors of the Rainbow	Jennifer Moore-Mallinos	Diversity	All
One	Kathryn Otoshi	Racism	All
Fly Away Home	Even Bunting	Homelessness	All
The Perfect Orange: A Tale From Ethiopia	Frank P. Araujo	Kindness	Ethiopia
Four Feet, Two Sandals	Karen Lynn Williams and Khadra Mohammed	Refugees	All
Each Kindness	Jacqueline Woods	Kindness	All
The Last Stop on Market Street	Matt de la Peña	Poverty	All
Golden Domes and Silver Lanterns	Hena Khan	Traditions	Muslim
Under the Ramadan Moon	Silvia Whitman	Traditions	Muslim
One Green Apple	Eve Bunting	Newcomers	Muslim
I Love My Hair	Natasha Anastasia Tarpley	Cultural pride	African American
The Magic Beads	Susin Nielsen-Fernlund	Mother and child living in a shelter	All
Just Ask	Sonia SotoMayor	Inclusion, being different	All

APPENDIX IV
High Yield Practices for Remote Learning

Whether students and teachers are in the same physical space or working remotely, the Reading & Writing Workshop Model offers a way to differentiate instruction and include student choice. The flexibility of the model lends itself to inviting families' assets, home languages, and cultures when teachers and students are not sharing the same instructional setting.

When working remotely, there are many effective technology tools that can be used within the workshop model to increase language and literacy. When thinking about which to use, first consider the overarching goal for your students. One common yet ineffective practice with tech tools is picking the tool first and then selecting the learning objectives or deciding how it will fit into instruction. Just because a tool is shiny and new does not mean it will support learners in academic success. Let's explore how we could take the Reading & Writing Workshop Model online by integrating technology into our established practices.

1. How do I teach reading and writing to ELs remotely or during distance learning?
If your school is closed and instruction must continue, working remotely with ELs will be just as important as it was face to face. Key factors to remember during remote learning are connection, clarity, choice, and voice. Connection is first. If you have already built a strong relationship with ELs and their families, then you are one step ahead. If not, connecting with ELs and their families during remote learning is first and foremost. Reach out to families and find out how they are doing and how your school can support them. Things to consider will be internet access, technology, childcare, and food. Depending on the circumstances for school closure, some families may be struggling physically, emotionally, or financially. Next, let students and families know what the plan is for instruction. Clearly articulate the plan in simple and easy-to-access instructions that students and families can refer to if needed. Choice and voice offer students and families some autonomy in remote learning. Offering choice in what students read or write about and how they share provides them with a chance to select something they care about.

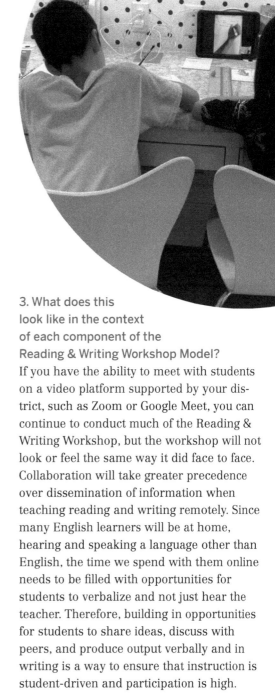

2. What are synchronous and asynchronous learning experiences?
Synchronous experiences are learning experiences that are done together simultaneously, whether students are together or apart. For example, watching a video together would be synchronous. On the other hand, asynchronous experiences happen at different times. We can take the same video and ask students to watch it at home on their own, then come to class ready to discuss with their group. In addition, during remote learning, students often engage in independent reading or writing on their own time, asynchronously.

Students that need the most support, either with language or with content, will benefit from synchronous learning. Some will need support with technology. They may not understand how to get logged on to the district platforms or where to find all of the resources. Other students will need support with communication. They may need help with the systems that are in place to turn in work, ask questions, and seek help. If you find that students aren't logging on, the problem may be that they need assistance with the platforms and technology.

3. What does this look like in the context of each component of the Reading & Writing Workshop Model?
If you have the ability to meet with students on a video platform supported by your district, such as Zoom or Google Meet, you can continue to conduct much of the Reading & Writing Workshop, but the workshop will not look or feel the same way it did face to face. Collaboration will take greater precedence over dissemination of information when teaching reading and writing remotely. Since many English learners will be at home, hearing and speaking a language other than English, the time we spend with them online needs to be filled with opportunities for students to verbalize and not just hear the teacher. Therefore, building in opportunities for students to share ideas, discuss with peers, and produce output verbally and in writing is a way to ensure that instruction is student-driven and participation is high.

Let's take a look at how each component can be implemented in remote learning online.

Mini-lessons and read-alouds can be modeled either live on video platforms or recorded and shared with students. Screencastify, Loom, and Screencastomatic are three common platforms for video recording mini-lessons. The benefit of recording the mini-lesson is that students who need to replay the video can replay it as many times as they'd like. While recorded mini-lessons and read-alouds are nice for replay, live video sessions with students offer greater opportunities for interaction. Teachers can read aloud from picture books, chapter books, poems, etc. as students listen and engage with the text. As the teacher pauses to think aloud, students are asked to type a response either into the chat or in their online journals. Some teachers create a shared Google Document for read-alouds and have students interact periodically during the reading.

One way to do shared reading online is by having students meet synchronously, either in small groups or as a large group, and view the same text while online. The teacher can either share the screen or make a text available to each student. Commonly used texts for shared reading are poems, picture books, and books on platforms such as A-Z Reading, GetEpic.com, and other online platforms. No matter what the text is, remind students that even though they aren't in the classroom, everyone will still all read together. Lead students in either choral or echo reading. As the class reads in unison, keep in mind that some students will not read.

Rather than calling them out, encourage reading and praise readers. Some English learners may benefit from hearing their peers and listening until they are ready to participate.

One key factor in holding guided reading during remote learning is that time is scheduled for small groups. Many teachers meet with small groups for guided reading on platforms such as Zoom or Google Meet. Typically, online guided reading lessons are flexible because students have varied access to resources. Some students will be reading from online platforms like GetEpic.com or A-Z Reading, and others will have paper books from the public library, the school library, or a home library.

Just as in face-to-face learning, remote independent reading takes up the majority of Reading Workshop. However, students can read independently on their own when they choose, asynchronously. It will be important to touch base frequently with English learners about what they are reading and to find out if they have access to books. Keeping students engaged in reading remotely can be challenging. We might be competing with playing video games, sleeping in late, playing with friends, and so many other tempting activities. Reading may not be a child's first choice. Flipgrid and Padlet are two technology tools that teachers have found to engage readers from afar. Students can post videos or responses about the books they are reading and share with their peers. They can also view what their classmates are reading and make comments.

The write-aloud can be implemented synchronously online using shared Google Docs or by sharing a screen with students. Some teachers have even modeled writing aloud by videoing themselves writing on a whiteboard as students watch. Essential elements to the remote write-aloud are that the lesson is kept short, thinking aloud is modeled, and students participate by chorally or echo reading the writing.

Even during remote learning, students benefit from shared writing. The practice of collaborating on a written text supports all students with language structures and building ideas on paper. Shared writing online is a synchronous experience and can be done by creating a digital space for students to gather "virtually" to write together. Some teachers, especially those teaching early elementary, lead the way by holding the pen or typing on the keyboard. Others ask students to do the typing. Collaborative writing about a given topic via shared Google Doc, in small groups or as a whole group, can be structured to support learners and hold them all accountable. For instance, each group can be asked to write on a certain aspect of the overall content while each student types in a different color. Modeling expectations, providing clear, explicit instructions, giving timely feedback, and chunking information will support learners toward success.

Finally, independent writing during remote learning is accomplished through choice, encouragement, feedback, voice, and by conferring with students online to support growth. Have students write on their own time, asynchronously, but touch base with them to guide their writing practices. If students know they will be sharing their writing with a greater audience, they are more inclined to write. Online platforms such as Bookcreator and WriteReader have been used effectively by many teachers during remote learning and in face-to-face classrooms.

4. What if students have limited access to the Internet? How can I support their language and literacy needs?

Teaching remotely is challenging as it is. But when students have limited Internet access, this adds a new level of challenge. Reaching out to families through mail, phone, and e-mail are options. If possible, share instructional videos through e-mail if students or parents have the option of viewing them on a smartphone. Many teachers have used choice boards with reading and writing activities that turn authentic experiences into learning opportunities. Choice boards are graphic organizers such as grids that offer varied learning activities for students to select from. Creating your own choice boards that target students' language and literacy needs is ideal, though many premade choice boards can be found with a simple Google search.

Reading & Writing Workshop During Remote Teaching

Literacy Components	Synchronous, Asynchronous, or Either	What this might look like online.	Teacher's Role	Students' Roles
Mini-Lesson	Either	Share a brief mini-lesson targeting an overarching skill either live on video or recorded. Screencastify, Loom, Screencastomatic are three common platforms for video recording mini-lessons. The benefit of recording mini-lessons is that students who need to replay the video can replay it as many times as they'd like.	Explicitly teaches a lesson to the group	Listen and participate
Read-Aloud	Either	Conduct a read-aloud either live on video or recorded and share with students. Screencastify, Loom, Screencastomatic are three common platforms for video recording read-alouds. The benefit of recording the read-aloud is that students who need to replay the video can replay it as many times as they'd like. While recorded read-alouds are nice for replay, live read-alouds on video with students offer opportunities for interaction. During the read-aloud, pause to think aloud, and provide students with opportunities to type a response into the Chat or in online journals. Create a shared Google Document for read-alouds and have students interact periodically during the reading.	Models reading	Listen and interact
Shared Reading	Synchronous	Have students meet online either in small groups or as a large group and view the same text. Share the screen or make a text available to each student. Commonly used text for shared reading are poems, picture books, books on platforms such as A-Z Reading, GetEpic.com, and other online platforms. Remind students to read together. Lead students in either choral or echo reading. As the class reads in unison, keep in mind that some students will not read. Some English learners may benefit from hearing their peers and listening until they are ready to participate.	Leads reading	Read along with the teacher

Guided Reading	Synchronous	Schedule times to gather online with small groups. Many teachers meet with small groups for guided reading on platforms such as Zoom or Google Meet. Typically online guided reading lessons are flexible because students have varied access to resources. Some students will be reading from online platforms like GetEpic.com or A-Z Reading and others will have paper books either from the public library, school library, or home library.	Listens and guides readers	Read
Independent Reading	Asynchronous	Touch base frequently with English learners about their reading. What are they reading? Do they have access to books? Provide students with access to resources and support. Just as in face-to-face learning, remote independent reading takes up the majority of reading workshop. Flipgrid and Padlet are two technology tools that teachers have found to engage readers from afar. Students post videos or responses about the books they are reading and share with their peers. They can also view what their classmates are reading and make comments.	Confers with individual students or works with students in small groups	Read self-selected books on their own
Write-Aloud	Synchronous	Model your writing on a Google Document, a screen sharing platform, or on a chart or dry erase board as students watch virtually in real time. Think aloud and write simultaneously as students observe. Keep the lesson brief and remember to stop to allow students to talk. Have students chorally or echo read what has been written.	Models writing	Listen and participate
Shared Writing	Synchronous	Gather students online. Share a document with them using Google Docs or Google Slides. Lead students in writing together. Elicit student voice in writing. Encourage students to share ideas for writing and periodically pause to read the writing in unison.	Holds the pen	Dictate
Independent Writing	Asynchronous	Encourage students to write independently and on topics of their choice. Meet often to guide students and provide them with feedback about their writing. Two popular online writing platforms for writing are Bookcreator and WriteReader.	Confers with individual students or work with students in small groups	Write on a topic of their choice on their own

References

Ascenzi-Moreno, L. (2018). Translanguaging and Responsive Assessment adaptations: Emergent bilingual readers through the lens of possibility. *National Council of Teachers of English, 95*(6), 355-368.

Ashton-Warner, S. (1963). *Teacher.* New York: Simon & Schuster.

Atwell, N. (1987). *In the middle: New writing, reading, and learning with adolescents.* Portsmouth, NJ: Heinemann.

Atwell, N. (1998). *In the Middle: New understandings about writing, reading, and learning.* 2nd ed. Portsmouth, NH: Heinemann.

Beers, G. K., & Probst, R. E. (2017). *Disrupting thinking: why how we read matters.* New York, NY: Scholastic Inc.

Biemiller, A. (2014, October 30). Oral Comprehension Sets the Ceiling on Reading Comprehension. Retrieved April 3, 2019, from https://www.aft.org/periodical/american-educator/spring-2003/oral-comprehension-sets-ceiling-reading

Bigelman, L. G., & Peterson, D. S. (2016). *No more reading instruction without differentiation.* Portsmouth, NH: Heinemann.

Bear, D., Invernizzi, M., Templeton, S., & Johnston, F. (2004). *Words their way: Word study for phonics, vocabulary, and spelling instruction.* Upper Saddle River, NJ: Pearson/Merrill/Prentice Hall.

Beers, K. (2003). *When kids can't read: What teachers can do.* Portsmouth, NH: Heinemann.

Beers, G. K., & Probst, R. E. (2017). *Disrupting thinking: why how we read matters.* New York, NY: Scholastic Inc.

Bishop, R. (1990). Mirrors, windows, and sliding glass doors. *Perspectives: Choosing and Using Books for the Classroom* 6(3). Accessed from https://scenicregional.org/wp-content/uploads/2017/08/Mirrors-Windows-and-Sliding-Glass-Doors.pdf

Calkins, L., Tolan, K., Mooney, J., Smith, K., & Marron, A. (2015). Portsmouth, NH: Heinemann.

Calkins, L. (2000). *The art of teaching reading.* New York: Pearson.

Calkins, L. (1986). *The art of teaching writing.* New York: Pearson.

Calhoun, E.F. (1999). *Teaching beginning reading and writing with the picture word inductive model.* Alexandria, Virginia: ASCD.

Carle, E. (2014). *The very hungry caterpillar.* New York: Puffin Books.

Clay, M. (1993). *Reading recovery: A handbook.* Portsmouth, NH: Heinemann.

Clay, M. (1991). *Becoming literate: The construction of inner control.* Portsmouth, NH: Heinemann.

Clay, M. (1985). *The early detection of reading difficulties*. Portsmouth, NH: Heinemann.

Clay, M. (1982). *Observing young readers: Selected papers*. Exeter, NH: Heinemann.
Clay, M. (1979). *Reading: The patterning of complex behavior*. Auckland, New Zealand: Heinemann.

Cleary, B. (1968). *Ramona the pest*. New York: Scholastic Inc.

Cooper, J. & Kiger, N. (2000). *Literacy: Helping children construct literacy*. Boston: Houghton Mifflin Harcourt.

Cooper, J. (2000). *Literacy: Helping children construct meaning*. Boston: Houghton Mifflin Harcourt.

Cowley, J. (1990). *Dan, the flying man*. Bothell, WA: The Wright Group.

Cowley, J. (2001). *The hungry giant*. Auckland, NZ: Shortland Publications.

Cronin, D. (2000). *Click, clack, moo: Cows that type*. New York: Simon & Schuster.

Cunningham, A., & Zibulsky, J. (2014). *Book smart: How to develop and support successful, motivated readers*. New York: Oxford University Press.

Cunningham, P. & Allington, R. (2011). *Classrooms that work: They can all read and write*. Boston: Allyn & Bacon/Pearson.

Delpit, L. (1995). *Other people's children: Cultural conflict in the classroom*. New York: The New Press.

Delpit, L. (1986). Skills and other dilemmas of a progressive black educator. *Harvard Educational Review, 56* (4), 379-386.
Demi (1990). *The empty pot*. New York: Henry Holt & Co.

Echevarria, J. & Graves, A. (2003). *Sheltered content instruction: Teaching English-language learners with diverse abilities*. Boston: Allyn & Bacon.

Ferlazzo, L. & Sypnieski, K. (2018). *The ELL teacher's toolbox: Hundreds of practical ideas to support your students*. San Francisco, CA: Jossey-Bass.

Fletcher, R. & Portalupi, J. (2001). *Writing workshop: The essential guide*. Portsmouth, NH: Heinemann.

Flower, L. & Hayes, J. (1981). A cognitive process theory of writing. *College Composition and Communication, 32*, 365-387.

Fountas, I. & Pinnell, G. (2017). *Guided reading: Responsive teaching across the grades*. Portsmouth, NH: Heinemann.

Fountas, I. & Pinnell, G. (1996). *Guided reading: Good first teaching for all children*. Portsmouth, NH: Heinemann.

Fountas, I. & Pinnell, G. (2001). *Guided readers and writers: Teaching comprehension, genre, and content literacy*. Portsmouth, NH: Heinemann.

Fox, B. (2004). *Word identification strategies: Phonics from a new perspective.* Upper Saddle River, NJ: Merrill/Prentice Hall.

Freeman, D. & Freeman, Y. (2000). *Teaching reading in multilingual classrooms.* Portsmouth, NH: Heinemann.

Fu, D. & Lamme, L. (2002). Assessment through conversation. *Language Arts, 79,* 241-250.

Gallagher, K. (2011). *Write like this: Teaching real-world writing through modeling and mentor texts.* Portland, ME: Stenhouse Publishers.

Gallagher, K. (2009). *Readicide: How schools are killing reading and what you can do about it.* Portland, ME: Stenhouse Publishers.

Goldenberg, C. N., & Coleman, R. (2010). *Promoting academic achievement among English learners: A guide to the research.* Thousand Oaks, CA: Corwin Press.

González, N., Moll, L., & Amanti, C. (2005). *Funds of knowledge: Theorizing practices in households, communities, and classrooms.* Mahwah, NJ: Lawrence Erlbaum Associates.

Gonzalez, V. (2016). Elementary English Language Learners. Retrieved from https://elementaryenglishlanguagelearners. weebly.com/.

Graves, D. (1983). *Writing: Teachers and children at work.* Portsmouth, NH: Heinemann.

Graves, D. (1994). *A fresh look at writing.* Portsmouth, NH: Heinemann.

Halliday, M. (1975). *Learning how to mean.* New York: Elsevier North-Holland.

Hayes, J. & Flower, L. (1986). Writing research and the writer. *American Psychologist, 41,* 1106-1113.

Herrera, S. & Murry, K. (2011). *Mastering ESL and bilingual methods: Differentiated instruction for culturally and linguistically diverse (CLD) students.* Boston: Pearson.
Honigsfeld, Andrea (2019). *Growing Language & Literacy: Strategies for English Learners.* Portsmouth, NH: Heinemann.

Hoyt, L. (2000). *Snapshots: Literacy mini-lessons up close.* Portsmouth, NH: Heinemann.

Hunt, L. (1996). The Effect of Self-Selection, Interest, and Motivation upon Independent, Instructional, and Frustrational Levels. *The Reading Teacher, 50*(4), 278-282.

International Literacy Association (2019). *Meeting the challenges of early literacy phonics instruction* [Literacy leadership brief]. Newark, DE.

International Literacy Association. (n.d.). Retrieved from https://www. literacyworldwide.org/.

Kamil, & P. Mosenthal (Eds.), *Handbook of reading research (*pp. 255-292). New York: Longman.

Krashen, S. (1993). The case for free voluntary reading. *Canadian Modern Language Review, 50,* 72-82.

Krashen, S. (1981). *Second language acquisition and second language learning.* Oxford: Pergamon Press.

Laman, T. T. (2013). *From ideas to words: Writing strategies for English language learners.* Portsmouth, NH: Heinemann.

Laminack, L. (2017). Read Aloud Often and Well. *The National Council of Teachers of English, 24*(4), 33-35.

Marinak, B., & Gambrell, L. (2016). *No more reading for junk: Best practices for motivating readers. Not this but that.* Portsmouth, NH: Heinemann.

Martinez-Neal, J. (2018). *Alma and how she got her name.* Somerville, MA: Candlewick Press.

Mikaelsen, B. (2001), *Touching spirit bear.* New York: Harper Collins.

Miller, D. (2009). *The book whisperer: Awakening the inner reader in every child.* San Francisco, CA: Jossey-Bass.

Miller, D. & Moss, B. (2013). *No more independent reading without support.* Portsmouth, NH: Heinemann.

McGee, L. & Richgels, D. (2008). *Literacy's beginnings: Supporting young readers and writers.* Boston: Pearson Allyn and Bacon.

McKenzie, M. (1985). Shared writing: Apprenticeship in writing. *Language Matters. 1(2)*, 1-5.

Munson, D. (2000). *Enemy pie.* San Francisco, CA: Chronicle Books.

Murray (1972). Teach Writing as a Process Not Product. *The Leaflet* (November 1972),rpt. in *Cross-Talk in Comp Theory,* 2nd ed., ed. Victor Villanueva, Urbana: NCTE, 2003.

National Reading Panel. (2000). Report of the National Reading Panel--Teaching Children to Read: An Evidence-Based Assessment of the Scientific Research Literature on Reading and Its Implications for Reading Instruction. Washington, D.C.: National Institute of Child Health and Human Development.

Optiz, M. & Rasinski, T. (1998). *Good-bye, round robin: Twenty-five effective oral reading strategies.* Portsmouth, NH: Heinemann.

Painter, K. (2006). *Living and teaching the writing workshop.* Portsmouth, NH: Heinemann.

Pearson, P.D., & Gallagher, M.C. (1983). The instruction of reading comprehension. Contemporary *Education Psychology, 8,* 317-344.

Pearson, P.D. (1985). Changing the face of reading comprehension. *The Reading Teacher, 38.*

Peregoy, S. & Boyle, O. (2008). *Reading, writing, and learning in ESL: A resource book for K-12 teachers* (5th ed.). Boston: Allyn & Bacon/Pearson.

Randell, B. (2004). *Blackberries.* Boston, MA: Houghton Mifflin Harcourt.

Reutzel, R. & Cooter, R. (2003). *Strategies for reading assessment and instruction: Helping every child succeed.* Upper Saddle River, NJ: Merrill/Prentice Hall.

Routman, R. (2005). *Writing essentials: Raising expectations and results while simplifying teaching.* Portsmouth, NH: Heinemann.

Routman, R. (2003). *Reading essentials: The specifics you need to know to teach reading well.* Portsmouth, NH: Heinemann.

Routman, R. (2000). *Conversations: Strategies for teaching, learning, and evaluating.* Portsmouth, NJ: Heinemann.

Routman, R. (1994). *Invitations: Changing as teachers and learners K-12.* Portsmouth, NH: Heinemann.

Salva, C. & Matis, A. (2017). *Boosting achievement: Reaching students with interrupted or minimal education.* San Clemente, CA: Seidlitz Education.

Sawchuk, S. (2019, July 18). Influential reading group makes it clear: Students need systematic, explicit phonics. Education Week Teacher. Retrieved from http://blogs.edweek.org/teachers/teaching_now/2019/07/influential_reading_group_makes_it_clear_students_need_systematic_explicit_phonics.html.

Schickedanz, J. & Casbergue, R. (2009). *Writing in preschool: Learning to orchestrate meaning and marks,* (2nd ed.). Newark, DE: International Reading Association.

Seidlitz, J. (2019). *Sheltered instruction in Texas: second language acquisition methods for teachers of ELs.* Irving, TX: Seidlitz Education.

Seidlitz, J. & Perryman, B. (2011). *Seven steps to a language-rich interactive classroom: Research-based strategies for engaging all students.* San Clemente, CA: Seidlitz Education.

Serafini, F. (2015). *Reading workshop 2.0: Supporting readers in the digital age.* Portsmouth, NH: Heinemann.

Serravallo, J. (2015). *The reading strategies book: Your everything guide to developing skilled readers.* Portsmouth, NH: Heinemann.

Serravallo, J. (2018). *Understanding texts & readers: Responsive comprehension instruction with leveled texts.* Portsmouth, NH: Heinemann.

Shannon, D. (2000). *No, David.* New York: Scholastic.

Smith, J. & Elley, W. (1994). *Learning to read in New Zealand.* Katonah, NY: Richard C. Owen.

Snow, C., Burns, M., & Griffin, P. (Eds.). (1998). *Preventing reading difficulties in young children.* Washington, DC: National Academy Press.

Sticht, T. & James, J. (1984). *Listening and reading.* In P.D. Pearson, R. Barr, M.L.

Sutton, C. (1989). Helping the nonnative English speaker with reading. *The Reading Teacher, 42.*

Suits, B. (2003). Guided reading and second-language learners. *Multicultural Education, 11*(2), 27–34.

Swain, M. (1985). Communicative competence: Some roles of comprehensible input and comprehensible output in its development. *Input in Second Language Acquisition,*15, 165-179.

Swain, M. (1995). Three functions of output in second language learning. In G. Cook & B.Seidlhofer (Eds.), *Principle and practice in applied linguistics: Studies in honour of H. G.Widdowson* (pp. 125-144). Oxford, UK: Oxford University Press.

Teale, W. & Sulzby, E. (1986). *Emergent literacy: Writing and reading.* Norwood, NJ: Ablex.

Tompkins, G. (2015). *Literacy in the early grades: A successful start for preK - 4 readers and writers.* Boston: Pearson.

Tompkins, G. (2014). *Literacy for the 21st Century: A balanced approach.* Boston: Pearson.

Tompkins, G. & Collom, S. (2004). *Sharing the pen: Interactive writing with young children.* Upper Saddle River, NJ: Pearson Merrill Prentice Hall.

Trelease, J. (2013). *The read-aloud handbook.* New York: Penguin Books.

Varlas, L. (2018). Why every class needs read alouds. *ASCD Education Update, 60* (1).

Vygotsky, L. (1978). *Mind in society.* Cambridge, MA: Harvard University Press.

Woodson, J. (2018). *The day you begin.* New York, NY: Nancy Paulsen Books.

Wright, W. (2015). *Foundations for teaching English language learners: Research, theory, polica, and practice.* Philadelphia: Caslon Publishing.

Young, C. & Rasinski, T. (2009). Implementing Readers Theater as an approach to classroom fluency instruction. *The Reading Teacher, 63* (1).

About the Authors

Valentina Gonzalez has worked in public education for 21 years, serving as a classroom teacher, an ESL coteacher and pull-out teacher, a district ESL facilitator, and a district professional development specialist for teachers of English learners. Through these roles, she has supported students and educators and coached teachers on sheltered instruction and ESL strategies. Her personal experience as an immigrant from Yugoslavia and as an English learner fuels her desire to advocate for English learners and support teachers and administrators in their work with ELs.

Dr. Melinda Miller, a full professor, has been teaching literacy at Sam Houston State University since 2001. She currently teaches at the undergraduate, masters, and doctoral levels. She previously taught public school in the classroom and as a Reading Specialist for 11 years. After completing an undergraduate degree in Education at the University of Texas, she received her Master's degree in Reading from Sam Houston State University and her PhD in Curriculum and Instruction from Texas A&M University. She has published over 40 articles and presented internationally. She has been an Educational Consultant with Seidlitz since January of 2015.

CPSIA information can be obtained
at www.ICGtesting.com
Printed in the USA
BVHW021005100621
609275BV00008B/1737